American Military History: A Very Short Introduction

VERY SHORT INTRODUCTIONS are for anyone wanting a stimulating and accessible way into a new subject. They are written by experts and have been translated into more than 45 different languages.

The series began in 1995 and now covers a wide variety of topics in every discipline. The VSI library currently contains over 650 volumes—a Very Short Introduction to everything from Psychology and Philosophy of Science to American History and Relativity—and continues to grow in every subject area.

Very Short Introductions available now:

For more information visit our website

www.oup.com/vsi/

Joseph T. Glatthaar

AMERICAN MILITARY HISTORY

A Very Short Introduction

OXFORD
UNIVERSITY PRESS

OXFORD

UNIVERSITY PRESS

Oxford University Press is a department of the University of Oxford.
It furthers the University's objective of excellence in research, scholarship,
and education by publishing worldwide. Oxford is a registered trade mark of
Oxford University Press in the UK and certain other countries.

Published in the United States of America by Oxford University Press
198 Madison Avenue, New York, NY 10016, United States of America.

© Oxford University Press 2018, 2020
Published in hardcover as *The American Military* in 2018.

Library of Congress Cataloging-in-Publication Data

Names: Glatthaar, Joseph T., 1956- author.
Title: American military history : a very short introduction /
Joseph T. Glatthaar.
Other titles: American Military
Description: New York, NY : Oxford University Press, 2020. | Series: Very short
introductions | "Published in hardcover as The American Military in 2018." |
Includes bibliographical references and index. |
Identifiers: LCCN 2020026330 | ISBN 9780199859252 (paperback) |
ISBN 9780199859276 (epub)
Subjects: LCSH: United States—Armed Forces—History. |
United States—History, Military.
Classification: LCC UA23 .G638 2020 | DDC 355.00973—dc23
LC record available at https://lccn.loc.gov/2020026330

1 3 5 7 9 8 6 4 2

Printed in Great Britain by Ashford Colour Press Ltd., Gosport, Hants.,
on acid-free paper

For Mac Coffman, Jim McPherson, Marian McKenna,
Dick Smith, and Frank Vandiver,
mentors all,
who taught me about history, professionalism, and life

Contents

List of illustrations

Preface

Very few factors are as vital in shaping the course of U.S. history as its military experience. Armed forces secured England's colonies; forged the United States; expanded its civil liberties; preserved it from internal and external threats; created pathways to political, economic, territorial, and cultural expansion; generated employment; developed science and technology; spawned new businesses; and affected virtually every domestic institution. And as years pass, the nation adds to its long list of wars, operations, peacekeeping missions, air strikes, and related activities.

Several dominant themes have emerged throughout American military history. Americans have struggled to establish a balance between regular military forces and citizen soldiers and sailors and to allocate that military strength. That conflict, most powerfully in evidence from the founding of Jamestown through the War of 1812, has persisted to the present day.

Professionalism has changed over the centuries and the armed forces have struggled to achieve it. By the early twentieth century, the army created an effective structure but lacked a professional culture; the navy forged the culture but lacked the necessary structure. As mechanization and technology improved, many in the military resisted changes. The magnitude of two world wars forced the services to embrace professionalism, and since then professional obligations have expanded exponentially, pressuring commissioned and noncommissioned officers (NCOs) to keep pace.

The aftermath of World War II and the ensuing Cold War showcase the limits of power. The United States emerged from World War II with exceptional military strength, a monopoly on atomic weapons, and a home front intact, yet it failed to recognize the bounds of its military and economic power. This legacy has continued to the detriment of the military and the nation.

These four themes—the size and the allocation of resources of a standing military; professionalism; technological change and its ramifications; and the limits of power—have resonated throughout American military history, interacting with each other and shaping the military establishment and its use, for better or worse.

Chapter 1
Citizen soldier and sailor vs. standing armed forces

The earliest English settlers on the American continent encountered a world of unknown dangers, one that required protection. Yet what form that defense should take was an unsettled question. They brought with them a tradition of universal military obligation but debated the necessity of a standing army, an institution they disliked, even under external threat.

As the first English colonists clambered ashore in Virginia in 1607, passengers cracked open a strongbox to read the orders from company officials back home. They were instructed to form three parties: one to build fortifications, one to explore for gold and other treasures and a passage to Asia, and one to plant crops and mount a guard. The document also named the leaders of the settlement, among them John Smith, a soldier of fortune. With limited knowledge of the New World, company officials included a proven soldier to protect these colonists from the dangers of establishing a distant outpost.

Thirteen years later, Plymouth settlers adopted similar precautions. Even though local Indians appeared friendly, colonists maintained guards and trained regularly. A visitor in 1627 observed colonists form four companies of men, lining up three abreast and drilled by a sergeant. "They assemble by beat of the drum," the witness recorded, "each with his musket or firelock in front of the captain's [Miles Standish] door."

Since Henry II issued the Assize of Arms in 1181, Englishmen had assumed a collective responsibility for defense. The first colonists in Jamestown and Plymouth brought this notion of universal military obligation with them. Legislation in Virginia required all able-bodied men, 17 to 60, to own weapons and serve in the militia. In Plymouth, males 16 to 60 had to serve. All other English colonies except Pennsylvania, founded by pacifist Quakers, created their own militias based on local rule.

In theory, the militia offered an extraordinary security. As the population of each colony increased, officials could assemble a force that vastly outnumbered any Indian threat. It was an excellent defensive system with true offensive capabilities, and over time militiamen gained valuable combat experience. Since the militia tapped local citizenry for brief periods of service, it was also inexpensive protection.

Still, the militia system had drawbacks. Governors could call out militiamen for only two or three months per year, and no one could be compelled to serve outside the colony's boundaries. Colonies hesitated to cooperate with each other, diminishing their collective advantages in manpower and materiel. Service also disrupted work and income. Over time, local militia gradually evolved into training centers and replacement pools, from which leaders sought volunteers. Paid or conscripted vagrants, the poor, and even criminals filled remaining vacancies.

Not only did colonists inherit a sense of universal military obligation, but they also embraced a spirit of opposition to standing armies. The English army played critical roles in the English Civil War (1642–51) and the Glorious Revolution (1688–89), and this convinced Englishmen that a standing army in peacetime threatened civil liberties. The militia system enabled colonies to avoid a standing army by tapping citizens to deal with Indian troubles.

Yet these British colonies were extensions of European powers, and when those nations went to war, fighting spilled over into the New World. Between 1689 and 1763, Great Britain fought four major wars with durations totaling thirty-seven years. Colonists dealt with Indian problems on their own and did not see why they should assist Britain in wars that had little to do with them. These global struggles stirred up Indian problems, and with their small, dispersed populations and poor record of colonial cooperation, settlers had great difficulty raising manpower and resources for major military undertakings. The exception occurred in 1745 when a British army, navy, and colonial expedition seized the French fortress of Louisbourg, guarding the St. Lawrence River, but Britain returned it in the peace treaty three years later.

Tensions between the colonists and the British professional soldiers (regulars) complicated difficulties. The British employed linear warfare, a highly stylized form of fighting with limited resources and limited objectives. Without concentrated power and vast tax revenues, governments could not maintain large armies. Attackers had little hope of conquering populous nations, hence limited objectives. The flintlock musket, a standard weapon, influenced tactics and warfare. Flintlocks were lethal but highly inaccurate at ranges of seventy-five yards. At that distance, an enemy could launch a successful bayonet charge, so commanders positioned their troops in two or three lines to repel attacks and to concentrate volley-firing. One line shot while others loaded. It was also easier to control troops in compact formations.

An army like this demanded synchronization, and troops needed very extensive training. Replacements took a long time to prepare for battle. In the Age of Reason it made little sense to suffer high casualties in what would likely be a losing battle. Since limited resources meant limited objectives, they often seized a community or region and ransomed it back to the defeated side. The logical course for the losing army was to surrender and have its crown exchange those captives for enemy prisoners or ransom payments. Many British officers and men viewed colonial soldiers who did not observe such battle "etiquette" with contempt. In their eyes, colonial militiamen and volunteers were untrained, filthy, undisciplined, and disrespectful.

Linear warfare may have been effective in Europe where there were vast open fields and both sides battled according to the same rules, but Indians did not fight that way. Amid extensive forests, Indians relied on speed and surprise. They would strike, press their advantage, and retreat when they lost it, exploiting terrain and cover skillfully. Indians were highly proficient with bows, arrows, and tomahawks but preferred muskets. Colonists responded by adopting tactics that were similar to those of the Indians, attacking by surprise, utilizing topography advantageously, burning down villages, seizing hostages, and taking scalps. When the British attempted to use linear warfare against the Indians, the colonists considered it foolhardy.

The fourth European war—the Seven Years' War—was different. It began as a struggle over the Ohio River Valley's valuable trade and spread internationally. When the French and their Indian allies crushed pro-British Indians and erected fortifications in the region, the Virginia governor sent militia colonel George Washington with 450 men in 1754 to drive the French off colonial soil. Washington ambushed a French reconnaissance party, but overwhelming enemy numbers captured his command at a flimsy stockade named Fort Necessity. The next year, British officials responded with a three-pronged offensive: one toward Niagara, another up the Hudson River toward Lake Champlain, and a third toward Fort Duquesne. All three failed miserably, with Col. Edward Braddock's expedition into the Ohio Country suffering 68 percent casualties. Once word of "Braddock's Massacre" reached home, Great Britain declared war on France.

For the first two years, the war progressed poorly for Britain and the colonies, but in 1758 Secretary of State William Pitt decided to fight it decisively. He devoted a larger share of the British army and navy to North America and brought in first-rate commanders to direct campaigns. He also made an effort to gain colonial support, paying and equipping all colonial volunteers, respecting militia ranks, and promising to reimburse colonies for their wartime expenses.

That year the war turned around for Britain. A massive army, navy, and colonial expedition captured Louisbourg; a second drove the French out of the Ohio River Valley, and in 1759, another seized Fort Niagara. In the most spectacular victory of the war, Maj. Gen. James Wolfe captured Quebec, although he lost his life in the fight. In the Treaty of Paris in 1763, France forfeited Canada to Great Britain.

The Seven Years' War damaged Anglo-American relations. Colonial efforts dissatisfied the British government, the war generated a staggering debt, and Canada required military occupation. Parliament began exploring ways to generate revenue from colonists. From the colonial perspective, Parliament reimbursed the colonies for only 40 percent of their wartime expenses. Colonists would have to cover those costs and were in no mood to refill the British treasury.

Meanwhile, westward expansion triggered a massive Indian uprising in the Great Lakes region, leading to a new military policy in the colonies. To prevent further violence, the Crown decreed the Proclamation of 1763, establishing a line between colonial settlements and Indian lands. Regular troops enforced the divide, which meant that Britain now posted a standing army in the thirteen colonies. Rather than pay the traditional half pay to officers in peacetime, the British government decided that it would be more cost-effective to get full service from officers. The Crown also used the British navy to check smuggling and other violations of the Navigation Acts—laws steering colonial trade to England or other British colonies, thereby creating jobs at home. Both concepts, however, depleted the treasury.

To pay for the troops and eliminate the debt, Parliament embarked on a series of taxation schemes, including quartering troops at colonial expense. Yet colonists, accustomed to viewing their colonial assemblies as the legislative body that could levy taxes on them, protested, sometimes violently, and even staged a trade boycott.

Boston earned a reputation for its spirited defiance of Parliament. To silence critics, the British government transferred some regulars into the city. Most colonists viewed the presence of a standing army in their midst as an attempt to suppress their right to free speech. For the next eighteen months, the people of Boston tolerated the troops, but on March 5, 1770, a crowd began to harass some soldiers, and troops reacted without orders and fired into the crowd, killing five and wounding six protesters. This "Boston Massacre" by a standing army proved to many colonists that the British government conspired to usurp their civil liberties.

British authorities responded by removing the troops from Boston, and tensions eased. The calm would not last. In 1773, Parliament passed legislation allowing direct shipments and cheaper tea prices, but it also focused attention on the tea tax. Citizens in Boston disguised as Indians slipped aboard merchant ships and dumped the tea into Boston Harbor. Parliament reacted by closing the port and returning troops to the city. This time, locals behaved more aggressively. They began stockpiling weapons and ammunition, and militia units drilled openly.

On April 18, 1775, the British commander ordered a detachment of 700 troops to march from Boston to Concord to seize a cache of weapons and ammunition. On the village green at Lexington, a band of 70 militiamen resisted. When the smoke cleared, 8 militiamen had been killed and 10 wounded. One British soldier was wounded. The militia dispersed and the British troops advanced on Concord, where they found and destroyed a few cannons and meager supplies. By then, militiamen from surrounding communities organized resistance in numerous locations as British soldiers marched back to Boston. British regulars lost 273 casualties while Rebel militiamen suffered 93. The revolution had begun.

The Rebels fought for a clear objective: independence. They hoped to rally support for the cause at home and abroad, maintain a political presence in a congress to oversee these efforts, and employ military forces against British "invaders." Fortunately, the Rebels had experienced politicians in the Congress and state and local governments to mobilize and sustain the effort. They sought aid from traditional British rivals such as France. Despite their decentralized nature, the combined population of 2.5 million could provide sufficient troops, grow enough food, and produce much of the necessary equipment for the war.

The Rebels' end was to gain independence by maintaining an army in the field and preserving the Congress. Those two institutions symbolized the continuing struggle for liberty. To accomplish the task, the Rebels benefited from three distinct military forces. The Continental army was the backbone of the struggle. Unlike soldiers in professional armies, these Rebels embraced a powerful commitment to independence. The second group was the militia, which played a central role in the war effort. Rebels controlled most local militias, enabling them to dominate areas where British troops did not occupy and to harass enemy foraging parties. Militiamen also aided field armies and fought in campaigns, at times providing invaluable service. Finally, the rebellion received vital support from France, covertly at first and overtly by 1778 once France entered the war. Without all three armed components, the Rebels probably would not have won the war.

Several internal factors worked against the Rebels, however. The Army's resources and supplies were inadequate, and Congress lacked taxing authority to acquire them or to pay soldiers' salaries. Without a navy, the Rebels could not import certain war materials, nor could they disrupt the flow of enemy resources from England. Most Indian nations opposed the Rebels, as did Tories, who were a minority of the colonial population.

From Great Britain's perspective, the goal was to put down the revolt. Britain sent a large military force consisting of the navy and army, but its key officers hoped to limit the bloodshed and sought a negotiated solution. As the war dragged into 1777 and beyond, especially after France allied with the Rebels, Britain had no choice but to seek an exclusively military solution.

To achieve its objectives, Great Britain boasted the best navy in the world and an excellent army that it projected globally. Despite a massive debt, it had the capacity to finance the war and hire huge numbers of soldiers from various Germanic states (most notably, Hessians). Many colonists offered aid to Britain, too.

Yet numerous factors worked against Britain. It projected military power over 3,000 miles, an extraordinary feat in the eighteenth century. Once France and Spain entered the war, fighting extended globally, and both those nations had good navies that could challenge the British and interrupt the supply line across the Atlantic Ocean. A war against fellow British subjects upset many at home, undermining the war effort. Moreover, the task of suppressing the revolt required a combination of carrot and stick, yet linear warfare did not work toward that goal. The colonies lacked vital targets, and the terrain was largely unsuited to the British style of warfare. Britain could project power up and down the coast, but it could not occupy the rebellious states. Finally, many of those in power were utterly dismissive of Rebel grievances.

The First Continental Congress in September 1774 aired grievances; the Second Continental Congress, convening in May 1775, declared independence and oversaw a war. In its deliberations, George Washington emerged as a knowledgeable and sensible representative on military affairs. Tall and powerful, Washington projected the image of a leader. As a wealthy Virginian from an established family, he brought judgment and credibility to the cause, linking the South to the rebellion. Washington was also the epitome of a citizen soldier. He had a clear understanding of the military's subordination to the Congress.

Even though Washington accepted the job of commander of the Army, he had his doubts. He was not a great field commander or strategist and had never led artillery or cavalry. Yet Washington possessed a great capacity to learn. He made his share of mistakes but he grew from them, so that by the end of the war he was an excellent leader.

By the time Washington assumed command around Boston, 20,000 militiamen had poured into the area and the Rebels had inflicted 1,000 casualties at the Battle of Bunker Hill. Washington's first job was to create a standing army as the embodiment of the rebellion and the backbone of their military efforts. Yet public enthusiasm waned, and despite Herculean efforts, he had recruited only 9,650 men by the end of the year.

To preserve a large army, Washington needed high-quality officers. Too many did not know their jobs and failed to discipline and train their men. Washington counseled them on how to be a responsible and responsive officer and urged them to "impress upon the mind of every man, from the first to the lowest, the importance of the cause, and what it is they are contending for." The Army's greatest strength, Washington believed, was its devotion to liberty.

Fully committed to civilian control of the military, Washington patiently worked with congressional committees, explaining to one committee seeking to reduce expenses why he could not disband the Army for the winter months. Members returned to Congress, calling for an expansion of the Army.

But Congress had little power. It lacked taxing authority and could not compel states to fill manpower quotas. Congress printed paper notes, but with no reliable stream of funds, inflation became rampant and people rejected them as payment. Thus, shortages of equipment, food, and pay plagued the Revolutionary Army.

During the course of the war some people in Congress and the Army wanted to replace Washington. Many rallied around Horatio Gates, a former British officer, who did nothing to discourage the movement. When Congress created the Board of War and Ordnance in 1776 to handle mobilization, equipment, and supply, and installed Gates as its president in 1777, tension between them grew worse. This placed Washington in the awkward position of reporting to his subordinate in military rank who headed the board. Finally, in 1781, Congress shifted from a committee to an administrative department with the creation of the secretary of war and appointed Benjamin Lincoln to the post.

In March 1776, the British evacuated Boston, and several months later they launched a massive expedition to seize New York as the staging ground for future operations. Under directions from Congress, Washington tried to block the movement, but he nearly lost his army in fighting on Long Island and then Manhattan. Washington retreated to the north, while the British preyed on two forts in New Jersey, capturing one and compelling the Rebels to abandon the other.

Although Washington's army escaped, it sustained severe damage. As winter began to set in, Washington, desperate for a victory, slipped across the Delaware River and on Christmas night launched a surprise attack on the Hessian garrison at Trenton. Washington inflicted nearly 1,000 casualties, and the victory buoyed morale at a critical time. He fought again successfully at Princeton and then escaped. These triumphs probably kept his army together that winter.

For 1777, Maj. Gen. John Burgoyne proposed a British campaign from Canada into New York to seize the Hudson River and strike into New England, quelling the revolutionaries. Instead, Maj. Gen. William Howe launched an expedition against Philadelphia, home of the Rebel Congress. Leaving a portion of his troops to hold New York, he transported the bulk of his army by water, landed, and then defeated Washington twice, capturing Philadelphia. Congress had long since vacated the city.

In New York, disaster struck the British. A force of Indians and Canadians besieged Fort Schuyler but eventually lost patience and retreated. As the other command under Burgoyne advanced into New York, Rebels obstructed movements front and rear by chopping timber over the roads, slowing its march and creating a food shortage. In two battles, Continentals and militiamen defeated Burgoyne's forces. With no hope of reaching Albany and with food nearly gone, on October 17, 1777, Burgoyne surrendered his army.

The Battle of Saratoga marked a turning point in the war. The Rebels captured an entire British army, demonstrating an unanticipated degree of prowess. France seized the opportunity and signed an alliance with the Rebels, bringing the world's best army, a powerful navy, and vast resources to the Rebels' aid. Spain and Holland ultimately fought against Britain, too. Unfortunately for the rebellion, Gates, the commanding general, took credit for the victories at Saratoga, and his favorites received promotions ahead of Brig. Gen. Benedict Arnold, the true hero. Outraged over his treatment, Arnold defected to the British.

That winter, Washington's army settled into quarters at Valley Forge, Pennsylvania. Continentals suffered disastrous food and clothing shortages throughout the winter, yet the army emerged from camp far better trained due to the work of Baron Friedrich von Steuben. A Prussian officer who had served on Frederick the Great's staff, Steuben transformed training and discipline with Washington's blessing. He simplified tactics, tutored a cadre in the new version, and sent them among the commands to train others. In June 1778, Washington's "new" army saw its first action in the Battle of Monmouth. Initially, a portion was driven back, but an effective counterattack won the field, as Washington's army inflicted greater losses than it sustained.

Later that year, Gen. George Clinton, the new British commander, shifted the fight to the South. First Savannah and Augusta fell to British troops, and in May 1780 Clinton captured Charleston and 5,000 troops. Congress then sent Gates to alter fortunes, but his army was routed at Camden, South Carolina.

Just when everything looked hopeless, fortunes shifted dramatically. The British dispersed their forces for occupation and began demanding citizens take an oath of loyalty to the Crown. Those who refused suffered the destruction or confiscation of property. These policies drove many uncommitted inhabitants to the Rebel cause, and a partisan war erupted. Word that the British took no quarter at the Battle of Waxhaws, supposedly slaughtering those who tried to surrender, fueled the animus. At King's Mountain, South Carolina, in October 1780, a Rebel militia command crushed British Loyalists, marking the first step in a dramatic turnaround.

To assist the partisans, Washington sent a trusted officer, Nathanael Greene. Greene's subordinates coordinated with partisans, harassed British forces, and engaged in combat on favorable turns. Finally, at the Battle of Cowpens, Col. Daniel Morgan stood and fought, defeating the British army. The British general Lord Charles Cornwallis set chase, burning wagons to keep apace, as Greene led the British on a wild march through North Carolina. At the Battle of Guilford Courthouse, Cornwallis won the field but suffered heavier losses. His wounded army eventually settled at Yorktown, Virginia, while Greene returned south, restoring Rebel control nearly everywhere.

Washington perceived an opportunity. The French Caribbean fleet would be in the Chesapeake area late that summer, and with the French officer Lt. Gen. Jean-Baptiste Rochambeau, Washington formulated a plan to feign an attack on New York and slip down to Virginia, where a Rebel force of several thousand kept close watch on the British. To ensure cooperation, Washington borrowed $20,000 in gold from Rochambeau to pay his troops $10 each. Many of them had gone years without compensation. The Rebels quickly mounted a siege with 16,000 French, Continental, and militia troops and almost thirty French warships. The British navy could not dislodge the French fleet, and with resources dwindling, on October 19, 1781, Cornwallis surrendered his command of 9,000.

With the loss of a second army and mounting opposition to the war at home, Britain reduced offensive operations and began serious negotiations. The Franco-American alliance stipulated a joint peace treaty, and the French intended to grant Americans only the land within the Proclamation of 1763 line. Yet one American delegate, John Jay, initiated secret negotiations with the British. To drive a wedge between the Americans and the French, the British offered independence and essentially the eastern half of the United States, minus Florida and Louisiana. The Treaty of Paris was ratified in 1783.

Over the entire war, approximately 200,000 Continentals, militiamen, and sailors served, about half of them in the Continental army. At peak, Continentals in uniform numbered

25,000. Approximately 25,000 Rebels gave their lives, two-thirds to disease, and another 25,000 suffered wounds.

Against a population of 2.5 million scattered over several hundred thousand square miles and 3,000 miles from home, the British could never project sufficient power to stifle unrest. Opposition to the war at home made it difficult for Britain to continue the fight. By contrast, the Rebels suffered from resource shortfalls, but a truly dedicated army of Continentals, buttressed by some exceptional militia service, overcame the disability. Over the course of the war, leadership at all levels improved, and France contributed vital manpower, money, and other resources.

As Washington's army camped near Newburgh, New York, awaiting ratification of the treaty, trouble brewed. The failure to pay and support the Continental army had led to various protests and revolts, but this time officers threatened to disband the army and settle on the frontier if they did not receive half-pay pensions. Some politicians who sought a more powerful government and military enemies of Washington fanned the flames. At a meeting to discuss options, Washington expressed dismay that they would challenge civil authority after achieving victory. With a dramatic flair he completely undercut the protest. It was probably the closest the nation ever came to a wholesale military rebellion. Congress eventually offered officers five years at full salary, but without taxing authority, it never paid them. Enlisted men received paper money for three months and honorable discharges that were redeemable at some later date for bounty land on the frontier. Most traded them for life's necessities. Once the Treaty of Paris was ratified, the Army simply went home.

With a new nation established, Congress voted for a postwar army of 80 officers and men, 65 of them designated as "peace loving caretakers," along with 700 militia volunteers to serve on the frontier. Upon congressional solicitation, Washington regarded universal military obligation as the bedrock of national defense.

A regular army of 2,263 officers was "not only safe, but indispensably necessary" to handle day-to-day affairs. He also called for a national military academy to train officers and a "well-regulated militia." In 1776, Washington criticized the militia: "They come in you cannot tell how, go, you cannot tell when, and act, you cannot tell where, consume your Provisions, exhaust your stores, and leave you at last in a critical moment." Over the course of the war, however, he recognized the necessity of citizen soldier in a national army and a well-trained militia.

When the Constitutional Convention met in 1787, the Founders attempted to balance necessity with mistrust for a standing army. The president was designated commander in chief of the Army and Navy and of the militia, while Congress received the power to declare war and to raise and support military forces and the militia. Congress could appropriate money for the Army for only two years; the Navy budget bore no restriction. The Second and Third Amendments to the Constitution, ratified in 1791, further made clear the public's discomfort with a standing army. The Second Amendment stated, "A well regulated Militia, being necessary to the security of a free State, the right of the people to keep and bear arms shall not be infringed." The Third Amendment imposed restrictions on quartering troops in private homes in peacetime and wartime.

Congress created the cabinet position of secretary of war and maintained a small field force that was stationed largely on the frontier. That army, however, suffered two consecutive disasters against Indians in the Old Northwest. In response, President Washington hesitantly appointed "Mad" Anthony Wayne, a Revolutionary war hero, as commanding general, and Congress authorized the expansion of the Army, now called "Legion of the United States." Wayne trained his troops rigorously, and his legions routed the Miami Indians at the Battle of Fallen Timbers in 1794. The government then restored the name "Army of the United States."

To aid security, Congress passed the Militia Act of 1792. It required all able-bodied White males, aged 18 to 45, to enroll in a local unit and provide their own weapon, ammunition, and equipment. Militiamen could only serve three months per year and states would designate officers and organizations. Though the law made citizen-soldiers the backbone of national defense, it authorized no financing, no uniforms, no standardization of organizations, and no inspections to ensure compliance or training.

About the same time as Wayne's victory, western farmers protested a whiskey tax that Congress had passed, refusing to pay and harassing tax collectors. Washington secured nearly 13,000 militiamen for federal service, and he led them into Pennsylvania. This massive force broke the back of the rebellion and demonstrated the wisdom of a militia system.

Despite authorization in the Constitution, Thomas Jefferson, James Madison, and other Republicans were reluctant to build a fleet, believing that navies only got nations into wars. Legislation that established departments did not create a separate navy; responsibility for it fell to the secretary of war. Yet threats from Barbary pirates in the Mediterranean Sea convinced the government to complete three warships. To prevent harassment temporarily, the United States agreed to pay tributes to the pirates to protect American merchant ships.

Other international troubles drew the United States into the Quasi-War with France. Fervor to spread liberty from the French Revolution in 1789 ultimately pitted France against the major European monarchies. Despite internal pressure from Jefferson and others, Washington disregarded the 1778 alliance with France and pledged neutrality. Nonetheless, American merchant ships quickly became caught in the middle of the war. The Jay Treaty of 1794 eased tensions with Great Britain but brought them to a head with France. When French officials demanded a bribe to negotiate peace, an undeclared war on the high seas with France ensued.

In the early republic, defense issues and policies got caught up in the debate over the power and direction of the new government. During Washington's two terms and President John Adams's four years in office, political parties formed over various issues. The Republicans, coalescing around the views of Jefferson and Madison, believed in a limited central government with no internal taxes. Fearing that a standing army would suppress civil liberties, they preferred militias aided by a small army and navy for defense. Federalists, with Adams and Hamilton as leaders, sought a powerful central government with a strong standing army and navy for security. A large military force required taxation and power for the federal government, and officers' commissions were patronage for party supporters. Republicans were pro-France; Federalists sought strong ties to Great Britain. Amid tensions with France, Federalists passed the Alien and Sedition Acts to suppress internal dissent, along with legislation to re-establish the Marine Corps, which had existed during the Revolution, and to create a "new" army of twelve infantry regiments and some dragoons. Washington served as its nominal head with Hamilton acting in his stead. The "New Army," which extended patronage to loyal Federalists, was intended to discourage invasion and intimidate opponents of the administration. Wisely, President Adams sought peace. He repudiated Hamilton's cries for war and by 1800 negotiated a deal that diffused hostilities with France. Congress in turn eliminated the New Army.

At the polls in 1800, Republicans were swept into office, with Jefferson winning the presidency. Immediately the new administration launched military cuts and changes, but international realities ultimately compelled a policy reversal. Jefferson's administration reduced the army slightly and broke the Federalist stranglehold on the officer corps. Jefferson endorsed the creation of the U.S. Military Academy at West Point to train scientists and explorers and to secure future officer slots for young Republicans. Jeffersonians also slashed the Navy, replacing warships with small gunboats for coastal defense. Once trouble with Barbary pirates resumed, though, they reversed course. The expanded Navy was large enough to check the pirates, but when the Napoleonic War resumed in 1803, it could not protect American commerce vessels, especially after the decisive British victory at Trafalgar in 1805. In 1806, the United States suffered humiliation when the British *Leopard* fired on the USS *Chesapeake* in American territorial waters, killing and wounding twenty and impressing four sailors as British deserters. The United States was too weak to retaliate.

While British warships harassed and impounded American merchant ships and cargo and impressed approximately 6,000 seamen, Jefferson and his successor Madison sought peace. Jefferson barred ships from trading abroad, causing severe economic hardship; Madison only prohibited foreign trade with Great Britain or France. On the frontier, an Indian uprising led by a Shawnee named Tecumseh heightened tensions with Britain. The United States sent Maj. Gen. William Henry Harrison to treat with or fight the Indians. With Tecumseh absent, the Confederation of Indians attacked the U.S. forces and was repulsed at Tippecanoe in 1811.

Many believed that the British armed Tecumseh's people, and frontier congressmen called War Hawks, led by Henry Clay of Kentucky and John C. Calhoun of South Carolina, clamored for war. Other Republicans in Congress refused to endure any more humiliations. Madison could not resist the tide, and in 1812 he requested a declaration of war. Seventeen days later, a divided Congress approved it.

At the start of the war, the U.S. Navy had seventeen ships, with no ships of the line and only seven frigates. The War Department

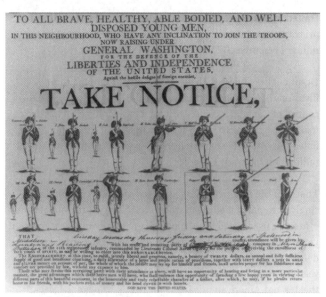

1. A 1798 broadside recruits new soldiers to the Continental Army. The Napoleonic Wars in Europe resulted in heightened tensions and a quasi-war at sea between the United States and France. In response, Congress authorized a significant increase in the size of the regular army—a move also meant to discourage invasion and intimidate opponents of the Adams administration.

was in a "wretched, deplorably wretched condition," wrote a War Hawk. Jefferson had expanded the army to 6,000, renewed construction of coastal fortifications, and allocated money for militia equipment purchases, but he had also sold the artillery horses and disbanded the quartermaster and commissary departments. In the months before the declaration, Congress re-established these departments and offered bounties to expand the regular army and to raise 175,000 volunteers. By comparison, Great Britain was already deeply involved in war for most of the last two decades. It boasted 237 ships, with more than 100 ships of the line. Great Britain had double the White population of the

United States and a far greater industrial capacity. Yet Britain's priority was war in Europe, where it committed most of its military resources.

Despite its weaknesses, the United States attempted three invasions of Canada that first year. If the United States seized control of Canada, it could use it for a bargaining chip to secure maritime rights or to retain it in the treaty. All three operations failed miserably due to poor leadership and the unwillingness of militiamen to invade Canada.

That year the American Navy achieved great success. Sailing singly or in pairs, it engaged when the odds were reasonable and otherwise used speed to escape. U.S. warships won five significant victories in 1812, buoying public morale when the army suffered defeats. The Navy's success on the high seas diminished the next year as Britain redirected more warships to the North American theater, but American privateers picked up some of the slack. These vessels raided British merchant ships and their cargoes extensively in both years.

The campaigns of 1813 focused on and around Lakes Erie and Ontario, which invading armies needed to transport supplies for the troops. The critical fighting took place around Lake Erie, where Commodore Oliver Hazard Perry frantically completed construction of four vessels on the lake, giving him nine warships. In September, Perry engaged six British ships, destroying or capturing them while suffering heavy losses to his own fleet. With Lake Erie in American control, the door was open for an advance by Harrison. In October at the Battle of the River Thames, Harrison and 3,000 men crushed a British-Indian force of 1,300. Among the dead was Tecumseh.

By 1814, with Napoleon staring at defeat, Great Britain sent 20,000 reinforcements to North America to launch three major offensives. The first, a naval expedition with 4,500 troops, advanced up the Chesapeake Bay in August, targeting Washington, D.C., and Baltimore. Brushing aside militiamen, British troops torched the Executive Mansion and numerous other government buildings. They then attacked Baltimore, where militiamen checked the British land force, and the next day Fort McHenry withstood a British bombardment. The British then withdrew, both sides suffering light casualties. Francis Scott Key observed the bombardment and penned the "Star-Spangled Banner" in honor of Fort McHenry's defense.

The second major British offensive pushed down from Canada into New York along Lake Champlain. Without control of the lake, the British could not sustain their land forces, and they built a small fleet to defeat the American one under Lt. Thomas Macdonough. Although outgunned, Macdonough positioned his vessels to neutralize the superior range of British guns. He also benefited from the wind and rigged his 26-gun USS *Saratoga* so that he could spin the ship and quickly fire the other broadside. In the battle, Macdonough destroyed the British fleet, ensuring the failure of the campaign.

During 1814, U.S. regulars fought superbly in the Niagara region, demonstrating their vast improvements. Across the river in Canada, at the Battle of Chippawa in July, Brig. Gen. Winfield Scott defeated an equal number of British regulars. Three weeks later, regulars fought a larger British force to a standstill at Lundy's Lane.

Yet it was a command of citizen soldier under Maj. Gen. Andrew Jackson who achieved the most extraordinary victory. In December 1814, in defense of New Orleans, he cobbled together a 5,000-man force of Kentucky and Tennessee militiamen, locals including free Blacks, and Jean Lafitte's pirates. Some 6,000 British under Sir Edward Michael Pakenham attacked on January 8, 1815. Skilled American marksmen repelled the initial assault by inexperienced soldiers, and when Pakenham hurled his crack

2. During the Battle of New Orleans, American soldiers, African Americans, and irregulars led by General Andrew Jackson fire at the advancing British forces. The American victory reinforced public perceptions of the merits of citizen soldier, despite their uneven service.

troops into combat, they too suffered devastating losses. Jackson suffered 62 casualties; British losses totaled more than 2,000, including Pakenham.

The lopsided victory at New Orleans had no impact on the outcome of the war. Fifteen days earlier, Britain and the United States had signed a peace treaty at Ghent. With the defeat on Lake Champlain, British authorities believed it would take perhaps two years more of fighting to achieve significant results. A war-weary Britain instead dropped territorial demands and proposed a return to status quo antebellum. The British navy halted impressment and harassment of American merchant ships because the Napoleonic Wars were over.

The United States was fortunate in the War of 1812. Distracted by Napoleon, Britain at peak committed only 35,000 soldiers, about the same as during the Revolution, and 20,000 entered the fight in 1814. Since that time, the United States had doubled in land mass and tripled in population. Until 1814, the fight in North America was a sideshow.

More than 500,000 Americans served in the war, 8 of 9 as militiamen. Officially, 2,260 were killed in action and 4,505 were wounded. Another 15,000 died of disease. It cost the United States $158 million, excluding property damage. The war largely eliminated Indian issues east of the Mississippi River, paving the way for Indian relocation westward, and it spelled doom for the Federalist Party, which had opposed the war.

Survival in the war against Great Britain became a source of American pride. Many referred to it as the Second War of Independence.

Chapter 2
The struggle for military professionalism

In the aftermath of the War of 1812, most people accepted having a small standing army and navy in peacetime. The critical questions then became how the nation should develop officers who served in that army and navy, and how they should enhance their knowledge and talents for wartime service.

The year 1817 marked a dramatic transformation in the U.S. military establishment. After several individuals turned down President James Monroe's offer of the post of secretary of war, he asked South Carolinian John C. Calhoun. The former War Hawk seized the appointment as an opportunity to demonstrate his administrative ability and further his case for the presidency. As secretary of war, Calhoun linked a military agenda with nationalist policies, securing the status of the military in the minds of politicians and the public. Whereas Hamilton had sought a strong standing army to bolster the federal government and the Federalist Party, Calhoun carved a place for the U.S. Army and Navy within the larger framework of economic development and territorial expansion.

As secretary of war, Calhoun proposed nationalist policies of a high tariff and infrastructure improvements, but he viewed them from a military perspective. High tariffs would foster the growth of domestic industries that would increase economic independence in wartime, and tariffs would finance roads and canals to facilitate the movement of people, goods, and larger military forces. Coastal fortifications and the construction of more frigates would protect American commerce and strengthen national defense. On the frontier, internal improvements would speed troops to hotspots, and a more elaborate frontier-fort system would protect citizens and develop a local infrastructure to service the soldiers there. When Congress sought cuts, Calhoun proposed an expansible army plan that would maintain the strength of commissioned officers and NCOs and would reduce the number of privates to a minimum. In crisis, the army could expand to 20,000 by bringing in recruits. Nevertheless, a tightfisted Congress rejected the plan. Calhoun upgraded professionalism by creating the positions of surgeon general and judge advocate general to improve medical care and justice. He streamlined a confused command structure with two commanding generals and directed the flow of information along a direct chain of command from the War Department through subordinate levels. By linking the military establishment with national goals, Calhoun placed the Army and Navy on more secure footing and instituted important improvements.

The same year, Maj. Sylvanus Thayer became superintendent of the U.S. Military Academy at West Point. After studying at French military schools, Thayer guided the academy for sixteen years and instituted changes in curriculum and instruction that remain in place today. He emphasized engineering and the military art, established small class sizes with daily recitations and grading, and instituted the demerit system for infractions.

With an eye for talent, Thayer brought in high-quality instructors to teach at West Point, the most important of whom was Dennis Hart Mahan. A professor of engineering, Mahan authored numerous military books and treatises, was a disciple of Baron de Jomini's writings on Napoleon, and founded the Napoleon Club, in which instructors presented papers on warfare. Mahan's teachings influenced two generations of cadets. Collectively, Thayer, Mahan, and numerous other professors laid the foundation for the rise of military professionalism through instruction and inspiration, imbuing selected cadets with a passion to keep abreast of new developments worldwide, innovate, and strive for military improvement.

The definition of professionalism has expanded over time, and few eighteenth- and nineteenth-century officers would meet modern standards. But a profession is foremost an identity. Individuals perceive themselves as professional and others recognize them as such.

Within two decades of Thayer's arrival, a majority of the officer corps consisted of West Point graduates. That educational experience forged a bond and an intellectual foundation among some graduates that enhanced their performance of duties. These alumni read military books and articles, toured U.S. and European battlefields, discussed professional issues, improved weapons and equipment, and authored articles on military subjects. The combination of Calhoun's policies and the evolution of West Point laid the foundation for a more professional regular army.

Until the mid-1840s, the army's strength averaged approximately 10,000. Despite its small size, the army consumed up to 40 percent of the federal budget, and Congress demanded extensive service from it. Most troops were stationed along the frontier, with small numbers manning coastal fortifications. Although the army fought Indians or moved them across the Mississippi River, it acted primarily as a buffer between settlers and Indians, hoping to prevent confrontations. Yet its other principal duties—the construction of roads and bridges—undercut those efforts by promoting westward expansion and clashes with Indians.

Enlisted men came largely from the urban Northeast, where recruitment was easiest. Perhaps half or more were immigrants.

With housing, meals, extra pay for special work details, and monthly wages, soldiers earned reliable income compared to most unskilled laborers. A surgeon conducted a confidential inquiry into reasons for enlistment. In one company, "nine-tenths enlisted on account of some female difficulty, thirteen had changed their names, and forty-three were either drunk, or partially so, at the time of their enlistment." The author Edgar Allan Poe was representative: after a failed romance, he enlisted as Edgar Allan Perry.

Military recruitment was tied to the economy. When jobs were few, the ranks filled; in boom times, soldiers were hard to keep. One day, word of the Gold Rush reached Lt. William T. Sherman's camp in northern California. The next morning, officers awoke to discover the entire enlisted population had deserted. A posse eventually retrieved all the men, but without legal identification and over vast territory, desertion was particularly difficult to check.

Many officers found frontier service frustrating and intellectually suffocating. Tedious everyday duties and small commands impeded training. Congress balked at consolidation to permit training as unnecessary expenses. Supply shortages, too, plagued the army. "We are now out of cartridges," one lieutenant grumbled. "A fine situation for a Military Post on the frontier and in Indian country."

The pace of military advancement was glacial. Not until 1861 did the Army offer retirement benefits. Officers who refused to step down clogged the ranks. In 1836 the adjutant general calculated that it would take a second lieutenant 58 years to make colonel.

Nevertheless, some officers continued to build on that professional foundation at West Point. Along with self-directed readings, they studied Indians and their culture, which helped them deal with crises more effectively. Many enhanced their small-unit tactics on the Great Plains, the arid Southwest, and the Florida swamps. Frustrating though these combat experiences were, officers emerged with enhanced leadership, tactical, and organizational skills that proved critical in larger wars.

Those campaign experiences proved priceless when the United States embarked on an expansionist war with Mexico in 1846. For several decades the United States had coveted Texas and California. The successful Texas Revolution and the annexation of Texas by the United States brought tensions to a head. When President James K. Polk ordered the Army into disputed territory between the Nueces River and the Rio Grande, Mexican forces also crossed the boundary and on April 25 attacked some U.S. dragoons, killing sixteen. Congress promptly declared war.

Despite Polk's posturing, he failed to prepare the nation for war. In a war of invasion militias would be useless, and Polk relied on the Army and Navy and 20,000 state volunteers for one year. He hoped to seize the territory in Texas and west to the Pacific Ocean and compel Mexico to yield it by treaty. The limited war necessitated little mobilization and modest expense for the United States. Its biggest obstacles were distance, the Mexican army, and northern opposition to the war, which viewed it as an attempt to increase slave territory.

Mexico hoped to protect its territory and regain Texas. Its standing army consisted of 20,000 soldiers. Most officers were aristocrats, while the poor comprised its enlisted force. Mexico's population was substantial and through conscription it could raise a much larger army, but its treasury was empty. The Mexican navy was small and no match for the thirteen U.S. warships. Internal political tensions, moreover, hampered Mexico's military effectiveness.

Polk's initial campaigns sought to secure the coveted territory. Brig. Gen. Zachary Taylor and nearly 3,000 regulars defeated

Mexican forces north of the Rio Grande twice, at Palo Alto and Resaca de la Palma. Taylor then pursued the Mexican forces to Monterrey, where the two sides engaged in urban warfare— fighting from house to house. As casualties mounted, Taylor and his Mexican counterpart, Gen. Francisco Mejia, negotiated a truce and Mejia's evacuation of Monterrey.

To the north and west, an American command of about 3,000 under Col. Stephen Kearny marched from Kansas to Santa Fe. After seizing the city, Kearny pressed on to the coast, where he cooperated with the U.S. Pacific Squadron and gained control of California by January 1847. With 800 volunteers Col. Alexander Doniphan marched south from Santa Fe, seizing El Paso and Chihuahua, Mexico. Doniphan's men then had to trek 400 more miles to rejoin the U.S. Army at Saltillo and helped to secure the territory that Polk sought.

Still, none of these campaigns was decisive. Only the capture of Mexico City could compel Mexico to yield the land that Polk sought. After desperate attempts to find a Democrat to lead the campaign, Polk grudgingly selected Commanding General Winfield Scott, a Whig presidential aspirant, yet saddled him with unqualified political appointees as generals.

While Scott amassed 9,000 troops for his campaign—many of them coming from Taylor's command—a Mexican army threatened Taylor. Mexican soldiers captured an American courier who carried details of Scott's operation. The Mexican commander, Antonio López de Santa Anna, marched an army northward in February 1847 and with 15,000 men attacked Taylor's force of 5,000. At the Battle of Buena Vista, Taylor's hard-pressed troops barely repelled the Mexican onslaught, inflicting heavy casualties on the attackers but sustaining nearly 750 themselves.

Scott, meanwhile, seized Vera Cruz and headed to high ground before the yellow fever season began. Santa Anna, hoping to employ biological warfare against the Americans, blocked the U.S. forces 65 miles from the coast at Cerro Gordo. Capt. Robert E. Lee discovered an old trail that took him into the rear of the Mexican army, which Scott used to rout the Mexican army and secure higher altitudes. Scott's army inflicted more than 4,000 casualties, sustained fewer than 400 losses, and captured 4,000 small arms and 40 cannons.

With one-year enlistments of nearly half the army about to expire, Scott halted at Puebla, about halfway to Mexico City, sent them home, and awaited replacements. During this three-month pause, Scott imposed rigid control over his troops. A large uprising would wreck his campaign, and he insisted that his officers and men treat civilians respectfully.

Rather than attack from the east, Scott swung to the south of Mexico City, where resistance was lighter. He won two victories at Contreras and Churubusco, inflicting heavy losses. Santa Anna then called for a negotiated peace; instead, he used the time to fortify his defenses. After two weeks a U.S. negotiator, Nicholas Trist, ended the truce. Again, Scott swung to the west to avoid the heaviest fortifications and won two more victories in September 1847. The gates to Mexico City were now open, and as American troops marched toward the center of town, the government surrendered. Santa Anna promptly resigned, and it took weeks for Mexican officials to authorize new negotiators. Scott devoted his time to restoring order for the inhabitants. As he had done in Puebla, Scott imposed rigid discipline to ensure that his troops protected and respected the locals.

Just when negotiations began to look promising, Polk ordered Trist back to Washington. But after discussion with Scott and others, Trist elected to continue negotiations. On February 2, 1848, the two sides signed the Treaty of Guadalupe Hidalgo, which gave New Mexico, California, and the Rio Grande boundary to the United States in return for approximately $18 million. Although

Polk wanted even more territory, he sent the treaty to the Senate, which ratified it.

During the occupation, Scott ran afoul of Polk's old law partner, Maj. Gen. Gideon Pillow. Polk blamed the dispute on Scott and ordered him home. At his farewell dinner, Scott gave credit for the successful campaign to the junior officers who had trained at West Point.

The war cost the United States $76 million. More than 42,000 men served in the regular army, and 73,000 joined as volunteers. Some 12,800 died—1,700 in action—and 4,100 were wounded. Most deaths were in volunteer units and due to unsanitary practices.

With the addition of 750,000 square miles to the United States, the army was hard-pressed to man coastal fortifications and keep the peace between Indians and settlers. In 1853, Jefferson Davis became secretary of war, giving the army the boost it needed. As a former congressman, senator, and war hero, Davis convinced Congress to expand the regular army by two infantry and two cavalry regiments. To fill officer vacancies, Davis promoted on merit, advancing the best officers. He adopted rifled muskets and had the arsenals begin producing conoidal-shaped bullets called minié balls. Together, they extended the range and accuracy of small arms significantly. Davis then authorized the development of new tactics manuals. Unfortunately, their authors largely copied European manuals and failed to address the increased range and accuracy of rifled muskets. Lastly, he sent three officers, among them Capt. George B. McClellan, to observe the Crimean War, where they witnessed severe sanitation and supply problems, the lethality of rifled weapons, and the value of field fortifications.

The Navy also made considerable strides in the 1840s and 1850s. For decades the Navy and the public had debated the merits of steam propulsion. Resistance revolved largely around the dramatic impact of technological change. Steam would upset the long-standing social balance and hierarchy on ships, elevating engineers and others who worked with mechanical propulsion and diminishing mastery of sails. Ultimately, steam engines won the day, but not without quite a struggle.

Most officers received their appointments through political connections and rose through an onboard apprenticeship process at sea. The U.S. Naval Academy was not founded until 1845, and its graduates had just begun to leave a mark by the late 1850s. Promotion was slow: a midshipman in 1839 could expect to be a lieutenant in 1870. The quickest means of promotion again was through political influence. As one officer noted, a cruise in Washington, D.C., was worth two around Cape Horn.

In 1855, Congress attempted to alleviate the logjam by creating a board to eliminate unfit officers. It deemed 201 officers incapacitated for duty due to health or incompetence and recommended their dismissal or retirement, provoking a huge uproar. After protests, 139 removals held, offering advancement in the years prior to the Civil War.

Throughout the 1850s, naval strength averaged 7,500, below its authorized level. Standard terms for enlistment were three years. The Navy received help in enlistments from "crimps," brothel landlords who ran a kind of debt peonage system. Much like the composition of the Army, most sailors were immigrants, but the Navy employed African Americans as cooks and in other lower-level positions to maintain its strength. Congress capped the quota for Blacks at 5 percent. Due to space limitations, quarters were integrated.

Naval service was tough duty. Discipline was harsh and pay was low. In 1850, the Navy outlawed flogging as punishment, and with the advent of steam, wages rose for specific duties such as firemen and mechanics. In 1854, Congress authorized a 33.3 percent pay increase, which improved morale and retention somewhat.

Although scholars have proposed a variety of causes for the Civil War, only slavery was powerful enough to rip the country asunder. Since the Missouri Crisis of 1818–1820, in which the North tried to block the admission of the Missouri Territory as a slave state, a sectional dispute over slavery seldom strayed far from the national scene. Once Abraham Lincoln, who objected to slavery on moral grounds and opposed its expansion, was elected president, Southern states began to withdraw from the Union. As the Mississippi Secession Convention explained its decision, "Our position is thoroughly identified with the institution of slavery—the greatest material interest of the world." Seven states in the Deep South then formed the Confederate States of America.

Lincoln made it clear that he would not interfere with slavery where it existed, but that he must uphold the Constitution and protect federal property. In an effort to retain Fort Sumter in Charleston harbor, Lincoln sent humanitarian aid to the garrison, forcing Confederate president Jefferson Davis to act. On April 12, 1861, Confederates began shelling the fort, which succumbed in thirty-four hours. Lincoln then called for 75,000 militiamen to subdue the rebellious states, and the Upper South—Arkansas, North Carolina, Tennessee, and Virginia—seceded and joined the Confederacy. The war was on.

Sectional tensions were reflected in the military as well. While enlisted men had to serve out their terms, officers could decide whether to remain in the U.S. service or resign. Approximately one in four officers in the Army and Navy resigned and joined the Confederacy.

Not only did the Union keep most of the Army and Navy, but it also benefited from overwhelming resources. Some 22 million people lived in the Union, compared to 9 million in the seceding states, 3.5 million of whom were slaves. The Federals possessed 22,000 miles of rail, all the same gauge, which contrasted with 9,000 in the Confederacy, with multiple gauges and only one complete east-west line. The value of Union manufacturing was nine times greater than the Confederacy's. Two counties in New York alone boasted more manufacturing than the Confederacy's most productive state, Virginia. The Union also grew 70 percent more corn and 80 percent more wheat, raised 60 percent more livestock, and kept 270 percent more draft animals.

Confederates in 1861 counted on their own advantages. Slave labor enabled the Confederacy to put more Whites in uniform. With "King Cotton" valued at more than all Federal manufacturing combined, cotton could secure weapons and materials and leverage European powers into aiding the Confederacy. Fighting in defense of family, freedom, and property gave Confederates a motivational edge, and they believed Southern society produced better men and soldiers.

To win, Davis knew the Confederacy must convince the North that the price of reunion was too steep to pursue. The Confederacy lacked resources to defend itself everywhere; therefore, he formulated a strategy that concentrated troops along logical invasion routes. Large geographical commands would enable generals to concentrate substantial forces to repel invasions. Davis directed officers to deliver powerful blows near the border that would protect citizens and resources, punish invaders, and discourage future attempts to conquer the Confederacy. Though Davis's strategy would result in high losses, he believed the people would endure these sacrifices for independence.

To save the Union, Lincoln had to subdue resistance to Federal authority. He declared a blockade of Confederate ports, squeezing the region economically, and utilized diplomacy to keep foreign powers neutral. Militarily, Scott proposed a strategy that built on the blockade. He wanted to seize Confederate ports to serve as coaling stations and staging grounds for invasions. He also planned to raise and train large armies that would eventually drive through the Confederacy along major river routes, drawing supplies by water. Scott urged patience and a negotiated solution, fearing that major bloodletting would alienate Southern Unionists and require extensive occupation of a conquered South.

Yet as both presidents soon learned, war controlled them. Public and political pressure drove Lincoln to adopt an overland campaign against Richmond. Confederates under Generals Joseph E. Johnston and P. G. T. Beauregard routed the Union Army at First Manassas, with a combined total of nearly 850 killed and 5,000 casualties, shocking both sides to mobilize on a grander scale.

In May 1861, slaves took action and began a process that transformed the war. Three slaves who had worked on Confederate military projects fled to Union lines and were declared "contraband of war" and subject to seizure, and Congress endorsed the policy in the First Confiscation Act. Soon, slaves brought family members with them, widening the war against property and Southern society even more. By July 1862, Congress passed the Second Confiscation Act, permitting the seizure of all Rebel property, including slaves. That same day, legislation authorized the president to organize and use Blacks for any military or naval service purposes. Congress had cleared a pathway for Lincoln's Emancipation Proclamation—freeing slaves outside Union lines—in September 1862 and his enlistment of Black soldiers. It became a war to restore the Union and to destroy slavery.

Soldiers on both sides also escalated the nature of the war. The violence, the enormous number of deaths in camp, general wartime hardships, and strong commitments to their causes generated a powerful momentum for devastation. Resistant to discipline, both sides pilfered livestock and food from locals, plundered private property for personal comfort, dismantled fences for firewood, and trampled cultivated fields for convenience. A war of restraint and cautiousness morphed into a war of attrition and will.

The firing on Fort Sumter unleashed pro-war passions, as people in both sections rushed to enlist. Lacking supplies, many were turned away. Raw troops assembled at mustering sites, where officials distributed weapons, clothing, and equipment and banded them into state regiments and hodgepodge brigades. Yet as they came from across the country, they formed into divisions, corps, and armies that became potent nationalizing elements.

Each nation was compelled to draw on military professionals and private citizens to command troops. Most citizen officers knew little about military tactics or regulations and struggled to drill and discipline recruits who brought democratic values into military service. Regulars, Mexican War veterans, and West Point graduates understood drill, discipline, and regulations and rose rapidly in rank and responsibility. Even though virtually none of them had experience with sizable commands, current and former professional officers exhibited extraordinary capacities to lead and learn, and in most instances they handled brigades, divisions, and corps very well. A few citizen soldier blossomed into excellent commanders at high levels, but they were the exceptions.

Once that initial enthusiasm waned, Davis worried about the dissolution of his armies when one-year enlistments expired. In April 1862 the Confederate Congress passed the first conscription act, which extended service to three years and imposed a draft on White males between the ages of eighteen and thirty-five. Over time, the draft ages extended to seventeen and fifty and allowed soldiers and draftees to hire substitutes for them. Selected occupations such as government employees and clergymen received exemptions, as did a White male who oversaw twenty or more slaves, but that category comprised comparatively few exemptions. Substitution was terminated in 1863 and the slaveholding exemption was abolished in 1865. Perhaps 8 percent of the estimated 900,000 Confederate soldiers were draftees, but the threat of conscription spurred enlistment. Wartime needs, however, demanded more. In February 1865, the government authorized the enlistment of Blacks; not many agreed to serve.

To supply its troops with weapons and ammunition early in the war, the Confederacy confiscated them from fortifications and arsenals and captured them from Federals. Ammunition came largely from various Confederate arsenals, particularly the one in Richmond. Although the Confederacy never lost a battle because of ammunition shortages, the quality of its gunpowder and ammunition varied and caused problems in combat.

The Confederate government attempted to finance the war by creating a new currency, selling bonds, and borrowing money overseas. The gigantic cost of war and the massive infusion of paper notes without effective taxing policies—by 1864, only 5 percent of the war was financed with taxes—resulted in runaway inflation and nearly valueless currency.

To spur enlistments, the Union adopted a combination of bounties and eventually conscription. When enlistments failed to meet local manpower quotas, communities held drafts. Federal, state, and local bounties induced many to enlist, and draftees could hire substitutes or pay a commutation fee. The Union also overcame prejudices and recruited 180,000 African Americans for the Army and 20,000 for the Navy. Many were runaways from slave states who counted toward Northern draft quotas, helping to make Black military service more appealing to Whites. Thus, the Union used the carrot and the stick, raising 2.5 million servicemen, of whom 5.5 percent were drafted.

With its powerful agricultural and industrial base and efficient transportation network, the Union Army peaked at over 1 million

3. Approximately 200,000 African Americans served in the Union Army and Navy. Of their contributions President Abraham Lincoln wrote, "Keep it and you can save the Union. Throw it away, and the Union goes with it."

men and still produced enough food, equipment, and goods to meet its wartime needs. Northern women entered fields and factories when necessary, and farmers purchased machinery to replace manpower. In many areas Union production in a single year exceeded Confederate production over the entire war.

To fund the war, the Union floated bonds to the masses, printed paper money called greenbacks, and checked runaway inflation by raising the tariff, imposing taxes on "sin" and luxury goods, creating a national banking system, and establishing a progressive income tax. Union inflation peaked at 80 percent; Confederate inflation soared to 9,000 percent.

Confederate momentum from the victory at First Manassas in July 1861 quickly evaporated, and over the next ten months the Union won a string of successes. Its forces seized the Carolinas' coastal islands, and in February 1862, Grant's army and the brown-water navy captured Forts Henry and Donelson on the Tennessee and Cumberland Rivers, taking 15,000 prisoners and unhinging Confederate defenses in the West. Rebel forces abandoned much of Tennessee, retreating to northern Mississippi. After a bloody Union victory under Grant at Shiloh, Federal troops under Maj. Gen. Henry W. Halleck severed the trans-Confederate railroad at Corinth. To the south, flag officer David Farragut's fleet raced up the Mississippi River and captured New Orleans, the Confederacy's largest city.

In Virginia, a different momentum developed. In the aftermath of First Manassas, Lincoln called in Maj. Gen. George B. McClellan to command the army. A smart and energetic officer, McClellan organized and trained a large field command, instilling spirit among volunteers and raising public expectations. Unfortunately, his ego and personality flaws impaired his effectiveness. McClellan insisted that the Confederate Army in Virginia vastly outnumbered his own army and then discredited Scott into retirement. McClellan became commanding general, but he squandered the fall campaign weather. Privately, he disparaged Lincoln as *the original Gorilla* and held cabinet members in disdain. Lincoln endured the slights for the good of the cause, but it unquestionably affected his assessment of McClellan. In March 1862, the first clash of ironclad ships, USS *Monitor* and CSS *Virginia*, resulted in a draw, but the battle enabled McClellan to land his army at Yorktown and advance slowly toward Richmond. By May he had marched within sight of the Confederate capital.

Then, the momentum shifted. Maj. Gen. Thomas J. Jackson conducted a brilliant campaign in the Shenandoah Valley, scattering Union forces and delaying reinforcements to McClellan's army. After Joseph E. Johnston suffered a severe wound, Lee took charge. In late June, he and Jackson launched a bold but uncoordinated assault on McClellan's troops, driving them back twenty miles. Lee then routed a Union command at Second Manassas and raided Maryland to gather recruits and supplies and influence congressional elections. At Antietam, Lee and McClellan fought to a standstill. Although Lee retreated two days later, he restored equilibrium in the East. For the Union, the "success" at Antietam enabled Lincoln to issue the Emancipation Proclamation from a position of greater strength.

McClellan's hesitancy to advance prompted Lincoln to replace him with Major Generals Ambrose P. Burnside and then Joseph Hooker, but little changed. At Fredericksburg in December 1862 and at Chancellorsville in April and May 1863, Lee executed Davis's strategy and defeated Union advances. Lee's greatest loss was Jackson, a victim of friendly fire. Nonetheless, Lee then seized the initiative, taking 75,000 troops into Pennsylvania. Over three days in July, Lee's army fought a battle at Gettysburg against a larger Union Army led by Maj. Gen. George G. Meade. Although Meade's soldiers repelled repeated assaults and inflicted some 28,000 casualties, they failed to destroy Lee's injured army.

Out west, Halleck divided his command before heading east to become the new commanding general. In Mississippi, Grant struggled to seize the bastion of Vicksburg on bluffs overlooking the Mississippi River. An attempt in December 1862 failed miserably, and that winter and spring, Grant tried various schemes to get at the garrison with the help of U.S. Navy captain David Dixon Porter. Finally, Porter shuttled Grant's army across the river and back below Vicksburg. In the most brilliant campaign of the war, Grant fought five separate battles against two Confederate commands, won every one, and laid siege to Vicksburg. On July 4, 1863, 30,000 Confederates surrendered, along with 172 artillery pieces. Less than two weeks later, the Confederate defenders at Port Hudson gave up, and Federals controlled the Mississippi River.

In September 1863, after the Confederates routed a Union Army at Chickamauga, Lincoln ordered Grant to take charge. Grant brought in supplies and reinforcements and then watched as Maj. Gen. George H. Thomas's men charged up the steep Missionary Ridge, crumpling the Confederate line.

Lincoln had found Halleck's performance as commanding general unsatisfactory, and Grant was the natural successor. In March 1864, Grant was promoted to lieutenant general and commander of all Union Armies. Yet Lincoln did not give Grant a free hand. He and Secretary of War Edwin M. Stanton wanted Grant to remain east and target Confederate Armies as his objective, exploiting superior strength with simultaneous advances. Grant ordered every field command to move against Confederate Armies in May 1864, applying pressure to the outnumbered Confederates everywhere.

In Virginia, Grant accompanied Meade's advancing army. In seven weeks of fighting, the Union suffered 60,000 casualties, yet it was able to lock Lee in a siege around Richmond and Petersburg. When Lee sent a detachment to threaten Washington, the vast Union forces eventually whipped the Confederates. Over nine months, Grant slowly stretched out, severing rail connections and forcing Lee's army to suffer more and more. By November, these Confederates were living on 900 calories a day and recycling lead for ammunition.

Over the Appalachian Mountains, Maj. Gen. William Sherman functioned as an army group commander, advancing on Confederates with three separate armies. On September 2, he captured Atlanta, the industrial and railroad hub, assuring Lincoln's re-election. Sherman then sent Thomas back to Nashville, and in mid-November he began a raid through Georgia to Savannah with 65,000 troops. Sherman's army consumed foodstuffs, liberated slaves, destroyed anything of military value, and demonstrated the defenselessness of the civilians, compelling

Confederates to desert to look after loved ones. Twin victories in December crowned Sherman's planning: he captured Savannah and Thomas's troops crushed a Rebel advance into central Tennessee.

As Sherman's army marched into South Carolina, destroying much in its wake, Confederate soldiers around Petersburg and Richmond grew weak from malnutrition and desertion soared. Fear for loved ones, hunger, and the impending defeat sparked 120 desertions per day. Finally, in early April, Lee abandoned his field works and fled westward. At Appomattox Court House, Virginia, Federals trapped Lee's remaining forces. Grant gave Lee magnanimous surrender terms: Confederate soldiers could go home and would remain undisturbed as long as they obeyed all laws.

Lee's army had become the embodiment of the Confederate cause. Its capture convinced other field forces to surrender. Prisoners received parole on terms similar to Lee's men. There would be no mass executions or lengthy trials. Only Maj. Henry Wirz, the commandant of Andersonville Prison, where Union prisoners suffered horribly from starvation and disease, was tried, convicted, and executed. Lincoln never oversaw it, though. An assassin's bullet killed him on April 15, 1865.

The Union won the war because it harnessed its superior manpower and resources, converted them into military power, and focused and sustained that power until every facet of Confederate society, including its military, shattered. Much of the credit belonged to Lincoln, who generated that military strength, articulated national goals clearly, and maintained the focus and morale of the public and its soldiers, an extraordinary feat.

The price for an inviolate Union and the abolition of slavery was massive. Some 600,000 soldiers were dead, another half million suffered wounds, and illness debilitated hundreds of thousands more. Destruction of property and governmental expenses totaled $20 billion. In return for Blacks' contributions in disrupting the Confederate home front and serving in uniform, they received freedom and, in theory, equal rights.

Scott's great fear was correct: massive bloodshed warranted occupation of the South, especially to protect 3.5 million freedmen. Yet he did not anticipate the political ramifications of Reconstruction duty, nor did he anticipate that war-weary Northern citizens had little stomach for compelling Southern Whites to respect the rights of Blacks.

By late 1866, Congress expected 20,000 soldiers to occupy 750,000 square miles of land while implementing a progressive agenda that Southern Whites bitterly resented. A federal organization called the Freedmen's Bureau, partially staffed by Union officers, oversaw the transition of Blacks from slavery to freedom. The army was supposed to cooperate with bureau agents, and sometimes did, but prejudiced officers and soldiers found occupation duties distasteful and dangerous. A gulf developed between progressive policies and actual implementation, so that the occupying army often refused to help ex-slaves in need and sometimes openly supported Southern White leadership.

The Army also became embroiled in the power struggle between the conservative president, Andrew Johnson, and the radical-dominated Congress. Congress passed the Military Reconstruction Act of 1867 over Johnson's veto, creating five military districts in the South. Congressional laws also compelled the president to issue military orders through the commanding general and required Senate consent for removal of any appointee that the Senate confirmed initially. When Johnson removed Secretary of War Stanton, the House impeached the president and the Senate narrowly failed to remove him.

As Southern Whites regained dominance and returned representatives to Congress, they banded with Northern Democrats to retaliate against the Army. In 1870 Congress left the Army without funds for two months and in 1877 it failed to allocate any money for it. As part of the Compromise of 1877 over the disputed presidential election, new president Rutherford B. Hayes barred soldiers from intervening to protect Blacks from white civil rights violators, thereby ending occupation. The following year, Congress passed the Posse Comitatus Act, making it unlawful to use regulars as a posse or to enforce laws unless specifically authorized by Congress or the Constitution. Other congressional attacks on the Army stemmed from politician-officers who felt they were denied wartime promotions because they had not gone to West Point, a slap at professionalism. Most complaints were baseless.

At the same time, the Army was embroiled in Indian problems. The U.S. government relegated Indians to reservation lands, often gutting the basis of their society and culture in the process. When Whites encroached on Indian lands or pioneers provoked violence, Indians retaliated and abandoned the reservation. Once the Army quelled the uprisings, it turned over responsibility to the Interior Department, until the cycle of violence renewed. With no authority to resolve the underlying problems, officers frequently sympathized with the Indians they confronted.

In fighting the Indians, the Army adopted several operational approaches that proved successful. Against the Great Plains Indians, superb light cavalrymen, the Army employed converging columns in spring, summer, and fall campaigns. The objective was to trap and disarm them and then return them to the reservation. Although the timing was difficult to coordinate—a problem that resulted in disaster at Little Bighorn—it usually prevented the Indians from fleeing or dispersing. The Army also liked to campaign in the wintertime. While Indian ponies became weak from malnutrition, the Army hauled its animal forage and coped better with winter conditions. In the Southwest, Col. George Crook and his successors exhausted their opponents into surrender with unrelenting campaigns. Dressed for the desert climate, mounted on mules, and aided by the friendly Indian trackers, Crook pursued his foe relentlessly into surrender.

West Point graduates performed quite well in the Civil War at ranks and responsibilities well beyond their prewar experiences. Most officers who opted to stay in the army afterward suffered significant rank reductions as they moved from volunteer units to the regular army. At the same time, though, the army settled at 27,000, double the 1860 strength and paving the way for large numbers of non–West Pointers to acquire commissions. The officer corps was highly experienced, but expansion significantly lowered the percentage with a West Point education. While American society professionalized, certain elements in the army embraced the movement and others rejected it, breeding conflict and contempt.

Wartime losses, frustration over Reconstruction duties, and changing missions generated a greater interest in military professionalism. As commanding general, Sherman encouraged military studies and innovation among officers, pushed for new tactics manuals that reflected changes in warfare, and established specialized military schools to train officers for future assignments. Schools struggled in their early years to create sound curricula and secure high-quality instructors, and a few, like the Infantry and Cavalry School, had to offer remedial reading and writing for those who lacked academic skills, but by the 1890s the Infantry and Cavalry School offered sound instruction and training in commands with combined arms.

The U.S. Navy underwent a similar crisis of mission. After the war, it demobilized to prewar levels, and the decline of the American merchant marine stripped the navy of its primary peacetime duty. Into the breach stepped Commodore Stephen B. Luce. A Civil War navy veteran, Luce founded the Naval War College in 1884 to teach naval strategy, the first school of its kind in the world. Officers learned to formulate and test plans. As its first president, Luce developed a curriculum and stocked the school with some talented instructors.

The most influential faculty member proved to be Alfred Thayer Mahan, son of West Point teacher Dennis Hart Mahan. He drafted lectures that he published with a lengthy introduction under the title *The Influence of Sea Power upon History*. Mahan pointed out that in wartime, nations must view oceans as global highways to project power. He sought large warships that could concentrate and take the fight to the enemy, winning climactic battles and dominating the high seas. The United States could then project military power, import and export goods, and block its enemies from access to materials. To extend naval power worldwide, the United States would need colonies to serve as coaling stations for warships and a canal across the isthmus in Central America to move vessels expeditiously between the Atlantic and Pacific Oceans.

Mahan's timing was impeccable. Industrialization and mechanization had led to periodic surpluses and economic turbulence. Domestic producers needed new markets and access to raw materials. Mahan's call for a powerful navy dovetailed with economic demands for American expansionism. Yet this imperialism was not solely economic. A burgeoning ethnocentrism and a strong humanitarian vein convinced Americans to help their "little brown brother."

Americans empathized with Cuba's quest for independence from Spain. Some identified with the Cuban desire for freedom; others saw great economic opportunity in an independent Cuba; and many blamed Spain for wartime brutalities that journalists hyped in print. As violence worsened, President William McKinley sent the USS *Maine* into Havana harbor to protect American property.

On February 15, 1898, the *Maine* exploded, killing 260 sailors. Journalists sensationalized the event, erroneously blaming Spain. When McKinley issued an ultimatum, Spain declared war. To salve American consciences, Congress declared war but disavowed plans to acquire Cuba.

The War Department was abysmally prepared for mobilization. Congress doubled the strength of the regular army to 65,000 and called for more than 200,000 volunteers. National Guardsmen, formerly called militiamen, could enlist as entire regiments and some did so. But with insufficient stockpiles and little forethought, efforts to feed, clothe, equip, and train newcomers proved disastrous.

Commanding General Nelson A. Miles planned for a fall campaign, but Secretary of War Russell Alger ordered troops to gather in Tampa, Florida, for immediate operations against Santiago de Cuba. The buildup was a fiasco. Brig. Gen. William Shafter, a Civil War hero who weighed 300 pounds and commanded V Corps (17,000 men), was unsuited for the job. Journalists descended on Tampa and pestered him continually. Logistics were a nightmare. Troops lacked sufficient food and shelter, with most of them exposed to the broiling sun wearing wool uniforms for a summer campaign in Cuba. With no government transports, the army had to negotiate with private owners to secure them.

Initial successes came from the navy. On May 1, Commodore George Dewey's ships attacked the Spanish Pacific fleet in Manila Bay in the Philippines and in less than two hours destroyed it, opening the door for a landed invasion. Panic gripped coastal communities along the eastern seaboard in fear of attack by the Spanish fleet. By late May, though, the navy trapped the Spanish ships in Santiago harbor.

Shafter received orders to coordinate with the navy and launch a campaign to close Santiago. His landing, fifty miles to the east, was mismanaged. Some transport owners refused to let their vessels go near shore, and many animals drowned in the ocean. With no plan, unloading was chaotic, and mountains of supplies piled up on shore.

While Shafter met with the navy commander on board the flagship, Maj. Gen. Joseph Wheeler, a congressman and ex-Confederate general, led an unauthorized drive into the interior, bringing on a nasty firefight at Las Guasimas. Reinforcements turned the tide as Wheeler shouted, "We've got the damned Yankees on the run!"

The victory opened the route to the Spanish defenses along high ground east of Santiago. Shafter's plan called for a division to swing to the north, capture the fortification called El Caney, and then roll up the main Spanish line along Kettle and San Juan Hills while other troops stormed the center. On July 1, with Shafter ill, the plan unraveled. It took all day to capture El Caney, and the troops who advanced along the jungle trail got shot up badly. A U.S. observation balloon marked their course for the Spanish troops, who peppered the area below the balloon. Only a frontal attack carried the Spanish position and saved the day. The cost was 1,400 casualties.

With heavy losses, terrible supply problems, and sickness among his troops, Shafter considered withdrawing and restarting the campaign. He did not know that after years of fighting the Cubans the Spanish military was in worse shape. In desperation, the Spanish fleet tried to escape and was completely destroyed. With nothing to lose, Shafter proposed that the Spanish capitulate, and over the next two weeks they negotiated surrender terms for the Spanish in Cuba.

Meanwhile, in May 1898, Maj. Gen. Wesley Merritt set sail for the Philippines with the first contingent of troops, capturing Guam en route. As in Cuba, an insurgency in the Philippines against Spanish rule had developed a few years earlier and gained strength with Dewey's victory and the return of revolutionary leader Emilio Aguinaldo. The Filipinos sought U.S. aid in gaining their independence, but Merritt soon realized the Spanish forces feared Filipino insurgents more than the U.S. Army. The Spanish negotiated a battle with token resistance against the Americans to save face and avoid capture by the insurgents. When the Americans executed the attack, the Filipinos surrounded the Americans and Spanish.

In August 1898, the United States and Spain agreed to terms: Spain granted Cuba freedom under American control and ceded Guam and Puerto Rico to the United States, while the Philippines was subject to future negotiations. In December in the Treaty of Paris, the United States also acquired the Philippines, despite considerable domestic anti-imperialist opposition.

News of the American acquisition heightened tensions in the Philippines, and in February 1899 fighting erupted. The Army employed superior firepower and training to rout the Filipinos, but combat evolved into a guerrilla war. Maj. Gen. Arthur McArthur took charge and ran an effective but brutal counterinsurgency, with relocation camps, free-fire zones, excessive destruction, and at times torture on both sides. With the assistance of Filipino scouts, Americans captured Aguinaldo in March 1901, but fighting continued for a year more. The war cost the United States more than $600 million, with 4,300 U.S. and some 20,000 Filipino soldiers dead. Perhaps 200,000 civilians perished.

Poor planning and preparation took its toll. The marines at Guantánamo Bay and army personnel in the Puerto Rican campaign under Miles executed their missions skillfully with minimal levels of sickness because they prepared carefully. By contrast, massive illness threatened the troops in Cuba, and military leaders signed a letter to McKinley—leaked to the press—urging the removal of the troops before they died. The press and the public howled. In desperation, the administration transported sick troops to New York, where their misery continued. The government sent "immunes," soldiers supposedly immune to tropical diseases but who in fact were not, for occupation duty.

To quiet protests, McKinley appointed a commission to investigate military mobilization and inefficiencies. Headed by Grenville Dodge, a Civil War corps commander, the commission was a political dodge, remembered mainly for Miles's false claim that troops were fed "embalmed beef."

Still, Secretary of War Alger had become a liability, and McKinley chose Elihu Root, a New York lawyer, to replace him. McKinley wanted Root to draft constitutions for the colonies, but he achieved much more than that. Root professed the concept that a peacetime army's mission was to prepare for war. He convinced Congress to create a general staff, headed by a chief of staff who became the ranking officer. The general staff would coordinate among the bureaus, conduct research, and plan for war, all serious deficiencies in the Spanish-American War. Root ordered that all staff officers serve four-year tours in Washington and then return to the field, to make them more responsive to troop needs. He created the Army War College to train officers and to research and test plans for the general staff. With the War College in place, other army schools modified their programs so that officers received training at critical levels of their career to enhance professionalism. Finally, Root sought to upgrade the National Guard and improve coordination between the regulars and the guardsmen. An army for empire would have to rely on citizen soldier, and guardsmen were the best option. The Dick Act recognized the National Guard as the first reserve of the army and enabled the president to call up guardsmen for nine months. In return, the army standardized small arms with the Guard, opened its schools and summer camps to it, held joint maneuvers, and certified guardsmen for commissions in volunteer units during wartime.

The Spanish-American War highlighted a lack of communication and coordination between the army and the navy. In 1903, President Theodore Roosevelt established the Joint Army-Navy Board to bring together the leadership of the two services to communicate and to plan jointly.

While the changes in the navy, the Joint Army-Navy Board, and the Root Reforms provided an institutional basis for what Calhoun had initiated more than eighty years earlier—a military mission that aided economic and territorial expansion—the drive toward professionalism was incomplete. The navy did not create a general staff until decades later. The Joint Army-Navy Board failed to draft genuine strategic plans until the 1930s. And army culture was slow to embrace the general staff system, undercutting its effectiveness. It took the enormity of the World War I experience to alter military culture and initiate further changes.

Chapter 3
Technology, mechanization, and the world wars

The decades that straddled the turn of the nineteenth century witnessed changes that set a course for more professional armed forces. The navy adopted Mahanian theories on warfare and embraced the new global mission of imperialism. The Root Reforms strengthened the ties between guardsmen and army regulars, created a general staff to plan and coordinate, and established schools to train officers for various duties. Yet neither branch truly professionalized. The navy lacked the organizational structure to utilize professional advances fully; the army possessed the structure but its officers clung to a nineteenth-century military culture. It took the harsh lessons of World War I and breathtaking changes in technology and mechanization to compel both services to embrace a professional ethos and to translate it into military power and effectiveness.

The assassination of Franz Ferdinand, heir to the Hapsburg throne, by a Yugoslav nationalist in 1914 triggered the First World War. Outraged, Austria-Hungary (with Germany's backing) issued an ultimatum that demanded Serbia suppress all anti-Austrian and pro-Yugoslav movements within its boundaries. Serbia objected. Russia supported its ethnic kin in Serbia, and France pledged its loyalty to Russia. Once Russia began mobilizing, Germany implemented its modified Schlieffen Plan to fight a two-front war against Russia, France, and Britain.

The German attack penetrated deeply into France, but the Allies blocked it outside Paris, and a counterattack forced the Germans to fall back and secure strong tactical positions. Both sides then began building a complex web of trenches, multiple lines deep, protected with barbed wire, and with terrain pockmarked by artillery shells, stretching from Switzerland to the English Channel. To the east, Russia advanced more rapidly than anyone expected, but Germany drove it back and badly damaged its armies. Fighting eventually spilled over into Central Europe and even the Middle East.

President Woodrow Wilson called on Americans to remain neutral in thought and deed, but that proved impossible given the large number of Irish and German immigrants and their descendants. Most Americans felt a cultural and political bond with Britain and France, and Wilson himself was an Anglophile. To avoid economic hardships at home, Wilson permitted the sale of arms and ammunition, which benefited Britain and France. When those countries began running out of money, Wilson granted them access to commercial credit. The mounting debt in the hands of Americans convinced powerful bondholders to lobby for the United States to enter the war on the side of the Allies to protect their investment.

To counteract British dominance on the ocean, Germany employed submarines to sink vessels suspected of hauling supplies to England and France. By maritime tradition, these ships cared for passengers, but German submarines were too small to rescue the passengers and crew on these ships. Even though the ships carried contraband of war, Wilson naively insisted that neutrals had a right to travel into war zones.

Each time the Germans sank a vessel and killed numerous Americans, the public became more upset with Germany. Several times, Wilson threatened war and Germany backed down. In 1917, with the ground war stagnating, Germany decided to launch unrestricted submarine warfare against shipping to coerce Allied capitulation. German planners understood the policy might bring the United States into war, but they also thought the United States could not affect the ground war for two years. Moreover, the United States intercepted a telegram from the German foreign minister trying to induce Mexico to enter the war against the United States.

At the time, the United States was in the throes of the Progressive movement. Urban chaos, governments that responded largely to the demands of the wealthy, and a concern for moral decline led to a huge and diverse reform crusade to instill order and morality in society, businesses, and governments. Many Americans viewed the war by democratic powers as a moral crusade and sought U.S. entry into the war. Led by Teddy Roosevelt and former army chief of staff Leonard Wood, the American public established summer training camps for college students and businessmen. Attendees initially did so at their own expense, but by 1916, Congress allocated money to cover travel expenses. Called the Plattsburg Movement after the initial camp in New York, camps around the country trained 12,000 officers in 1916 alone and promoted preparedness.

The federal government moved more tentatively. Wilson's first secretary of war resigned over the president's lack of support. His replacement, Newton D. Baker, had better success. Baker lobbied for passage of the National Defense Act of 1916, which expanded the size of the regular army; required guardsmen to take a federal as well as a state oath, giving the president greater control of them; granted the president unusual wartime powers to control industry for mobilization; and created reserve officer training at colleges. Wilson won re-election in November 1916 on the slogan "He Kept Us Out of War." In April 1917, however, the United States declared war on Germany. Wilson viewed the Allied cause as a crusade to ensure peace, democracy, and economic expansion worldwide. In January 1918, without notifying Allied leaders,

Wilson detailed his postwar aims in his Fourteen Points speech. He called for armament reductions and freedom of the seas, the self-determination of minority peoples, and an international organization to resolve disputes and keep the peace. Much of the United States and Europe embraced the Fourteen Points, but Allied leaders rejected them. In response, the French prime minister supposedly mocked, "The Good Lord had only ten!"

Wilson sought the concentration of power in wartime in the executive branch. He exhibited little interest in military matters and delegated authority to his subordinates, while he devoted his energy to diplomatic affairs. For military strategy, Wilson placed responsibility largely in the hands of American Expeditionary Forces (AEF) commander Maj. Gen. John J. Pershing. Since Baker knew little about warfare, and the chief of staff and his two initial replacements lacked vision and toughness, Baker assured Pershing that his authority would be supreme. Pershing took it to heart.

Upon entering the war, the United States learned that unrestricted submarine warfare had proved exceedingly effective. Without some solution to the supply crisis, Britain would have to withdraw from the war by November 1917. Adm. William S. Sims, U.S. naval commander in Europe, convinced both Allied governments to employ convoys to escort clusters of merchant ships. These vessels could shield slow-moving supply ships and draw out and sink the attacking submarines. The United States accelerated the production and deployment of destroyers, submarine chasers, and merchant ships, too, and the approach proved successful.

Nearly half a million men and women served in the U.S. Navy. It was generally tedious duty convoying supplies, serving as stevedores, or scanning the ocean for enemy submarines. As one sailor admitted, "You'd almost be glad to see a ship sunk, anything to cheer up the monotony of patrolling."

Although Secretary of the Navy Josephus Daniels retained much authority, Sims oversaw the naval war. A progressive thinker, Sims set up an expansive headquarters on land and viewed his command as an Allied force. The decisions earned him criticism from the old guard, but both were sound.

On land, the Allies desperately needed infantrymen. Massive bloodshed depleted French and British forces, and both nations sought manpower for existing units. The Army entered the war with 133,000 soldiers and 185,000 guardsmen, a number woefully inadequate to meet Allied needs. In June the War Department rushed a token division under Pershing to France, but a general staff study estimated it would take twenty-six months to get 500,000 trained troops to France. From France, Pershing analyzed the situation and called for an AEF strength of 1 million men before the end of 1918, which he eventually raised to 5 million. The War Department calculated that U.S. logistics could only support an AEF of 4 million, though, and that the force would have to rely heavily on French and British weapons and equipment. The distinction between Pershing's demands and home-front capabilities indicated a fundamental problem with the command structure. Either way, the war effort would require unprecedented mobilization.

To meet its manpower needs, the United States adopted a two-track approach: volunteering and a draft. Wilson believed conscription was the only democratic way to raise a huge army in wartime, and of the 4.8 million who served, 2.8 million were drafted. Local draft boards oversaw the selection of men between the ages of eighteen and forty-five.

Nearly half of all officers received training at Plattsburg-type camps. Many of the others went to officers' training programs or were enlisted regulars or guardsmen who received commissions. The army limited Black commissions and nearly all attended an officer training course in Des Moines, Iowa.

The army began building thirty-two training camps, seventeen of them in the South. This proved problematic when local boards drafted African Americans in disproportionate numbers. With armed Blacks training amid White civilians, racial tensions rose and altercations ensued. In the worst of these clashes, a riot in Houston resulted in the deaths of two Black soldiers and seventeen White civilians. Nineteen Black soldiers were executed for their role and more than sixty received life sentences.

At home, the Black community largely embraced the war, yet Wilson cared little for African Americans and set a tone that reverberated throughout the army. Some 400,000 Blacks served mostly in support and manual labor jobs. Fewer than 1 percent of all officers were Black. Because White citizens resented the nearby presence of armed Blacks, training on any level above regiment was nearly impossible.

Severe shortages afflicted the army. Many troops were stuck in their induction clothing for weeks. They carried signs that read "Tank" but could not train with the real thing. Some infantrymen never fired on a target; artillerymen practiced servicing phony guns. Inefficiency nearly brought mobilization to a screeching halt. Congress was slow to allocate funds, the War Department failed to cut orders for goods and equipment, and military bureaus worked at cross purposes.

By early 1918, however, the crisis began to pass as necessity overrode the traditional approaches. George W. Goethals came out of retirement to serve as quartermaster general, instilling organization and efficiency. By the summer, the War Department had consolidated power and given all supply responsibility to Goethals. Financier Bernard Baruch took over the War Industries Board, gaining a stranglehold on raw materials and transforming domestic production for military needs. And Baker finally got a strong and efficient chief of staff in Peyton C. March, Pershing's chief of artillery. March galvanized the war effort, but he clashed with Pershing over troop strength, supplies, and promotions.

The Wilson administration sought to finance the war through a balance of taxes and debt. Many Progressives viewed this as an opportunity to create a more progressive income tax—and rates did go up—but bond sales funded much of the war. With the government more focused on productivity than on inflation, prices began to spiral upward, burdening the poor and middle class.

Wilson launched a vigorous propaganda campaign led by the Committee on Public Information. "Four-Minute Men" reminded the public in brief speeches about the causes, goals, and progress of the war. They promoted bond sales and voluntarism at home, including wheatless and meatless days. Laws forbade the consumption of alcohol by military personnel, fulfilling a Progressive goal of prohibition, saving grain for the war effort, and paving the way for the Eighteenth Amendment in 1919. The repercussions of propaganda were long-lasting: anti-German sentiments morphed into xenophobia, which strengthened after the war.

The War Department decided on a Square Division of 28,000 men, with the four regiments (hence, the "Square") organized into two brigades. With a shortage of proven officers and the distance from home a huge division, twice the size of allied divisions, made sense.

The Allies wanted the United States to flood Europe with privates. Experienced Allied officers would see that they received proper arms and training and then incorporate them into existing French and British units. The Allies thought the United States would waste valuable manpower duplicating supply, staff, and officer positions while the Europeans had experienced individuals who could handle the work.

4. The United States government called upon the people at home to support World War I through the purchase of Liberty Bonds. A poster advertising their sale depicts a German soldier looking threateningly across the Atlantic, his fingers wet with blood.

Pershing balked at the idea of amalgamation. The Allied plan would prevent the creation of an independent American army, hiding its combat achievements and diminishing its standing in peace negotiations. Many soldiers of Irish descent would not serve under British officers and few American troops spoke French, making integration problematic. Allied commanders, moreover, had squandered millions of lives. Pershing naively believed American officers could do better, including himself. Yet Britain held a trump card in transport ships, which it used to leverage a compromise. French and British commanders could use American troops in times of need, but ultimately the United States would create its own armies and occupy a portion of the line.

To improve cooperation, the Allies formed the Supreme War Council (SWC) in November 1917. It consisted of the political head of each country (Wilson's confidant "Colonel" Edward House substituted) and a military representative. Although the council made decisions, each country could appeal the decision to its own government. By early 1918, the SWC selected the Frenchman Ferdinand Foch as its generalissimo of Allied military forces. Since France contributed the most troops and Foch was a leading general, the choice was sound.

With the collapse of Russia in 1917, Germany was able to shift troops from east to west and launch powerful attacks against the Allies in early 1918. The Germans penetrated deeply, but the depth of defenses and the arrival of huge numbers of Americans buoyed the Allies and helped bring matters to a halt.

In late May 1918, Americans had their first independent action, as the 28th Infantry Regiment captured and held the town of Cantigny. Within days, Americans were fighting on a much larger scale at Belleau Wood and Château-Thierry, exhibiting the aggressiveness that Pershing had expected. Yet Pershing's open fighting tactics failed, and American officers adopted the tactics of

their Allies with greater success, relying on combined arms—
artillery, tanks, infantry, and aviation.

The quality and especially the quantity of Americans impressed
the Allies and the Germans. In an event that epitomized the
shifting momentum, some marines arrived on the scene amid a
French retreat. A French officer urged them to fall back. "Retreat?"
shouted Capt. Lloyd Williams. "Hell, we just got here."

The Army sent two separate Black divisions to France, the 92nd
and 93rd, and some units had Black officers. Both divisions
battled the enemy and prejudice simultaneously. The 92nd fought
against Germans in the Meuse-Argonne. Even though it fought as
well or better than adjacent White divisions, the high command
publicly branded the entire division cowardly. The 93rd had its
regiments parceled out to the French, and it fought superbly on
multiple battlefields, earning hundreds of honors. But without
political and military leaders who evaluated their service fairly,
Black soldiers never received the tributes they deserved.

By August 1918, the Americans organized the First Army and
planned a major offensive. In late September nine divisions
assaulted a salient at St. Mihiel. Within two days, U.S. and French
troops had erased the bulge, inflicting 17,000 casualties on the
enemy, with Americans sustaining 7,000 losses.

As a concession to fight independently at St. Mihiel, Pershing
agreed to launch an attack in late September in the Meuse-
Argonne sector. This required the nighttime movement of
600,000 men plus equipment and supplies into position and
shifting another 220,000, a monumental task that a brilliant
officer named Col. George C. Marshall accomplished. The attack
in late September made great headway initially and then bogged
down. Pershing, who oversaw too many duties, replaced himself as
commander of the First Army with Maj. Gen. Hunter Liggett.

THE AMERICAN SOLDIERS IN PRESENCE OF GAS - 42ND DIV. ESSAY-FR. 9-20-18

5. **Troops embroiled in the 1918 Meuse-Argonne offensive wear gas masks to shield themselves from the deadly German poison gas attacks. This equipment would protect against chlorine and phosgene but not against the blistering, maiming effects of other agents such as mustard gas.**

Liggett called a halt, regrouped, and then launched a new attack that again made headway.

Fliers in World War I were the antithesis of ground troops. While soldiers trudged through mud and shell craters against fortified positions, barbed wire, artillery, and machine guns, aviators soared above them and battled at high speeds against adversaries they could see. They fought dogfights, reconnoitered enemy positions, and even dropped handheld bombs. Their deeds captured the public imagination.

Four years after Orville and Wilbur Wright flew in North Carolina, the Army awarded them a contract to build an aircraft that could fly 40 miles per hour with two persons (350 combined pounds), remain aloft for an hour, and fit into an army wagon. The Wrights trained two officers, but when those temporary assignments expired, the War Department ordered Lt. Benjamin Foulois to take the aircraft to Texas and fly it there. Foulois learned to fly by correspondence. With little military support, he often had to pay for fuel himself and even invented the seat belt after he fell of the plane. Without much political and bureaucratic support, American military aviation lagged far behind that of the European powers.

When the United States entered the war, France requested 4,500 U.S. pilots and 17,000 planes, goals American leaders hoped to meet, but the slow transition in factories caused delays, so that by mid-summer 1918 only 78 planes had arrived in Europe. France picked up the slack, providing most of the aircraft, while American manufacturers contributed 15,000 high-quality engines and other equipment.

For pilots, the United States began training individuals at various universities and lured experienced pilots as instructors from Britain and Canada. In France, the United States set up a training school near Orleans and drew on experienced aviators such as Maj. Raoul Lufbery, an American ace who fought for France.

When Pershing arrived, Maj. Billy Mitchell met him at the Paris train station. A regular army officer, the son of a U.S. senator, fluent in French, and an aviator, Mitchell proved to be both troublesome and invaluable. Foulois soon superseded Mitchell, and a classmate of Pershing's took charge over Foulois, but it was Mitchell who held court. Flying French and British aircraft, Mitchell's pilots dominated the air in the summer of 1918, and on September 26 he placed 842 aircraft in the skies against the Germans. Mitchell took the war to the enemy rear areas and set the stage for his postwar ideas on strategic bombardment— bombing the home front to break civilian support for the war.

By mid-July 1918, the Allies had blunted the German offensive and assumed the initiative. With buoyed morale, overwhelming

6. An aviation commander in World War I, William "Billy" Mitchell became one of the leading advocates of the doctrine of strategic bombing. His outspokenness ultimately led to his court-martial and resignation from the army in 1926.

numbers of tanks, and an increasing American presence, momentum shifted dramatically. The Allies launched offensives in several locations and the beleaguered Germans could not respond effectively. Germany's allies, Turkey and Austria-Hungary, collapsed, and the prolonged hardships buckled German morale at home. The German army began to melt away slowly by desertion, capture, and casualties.

Mutinies, strikes, and battlefield failures compelled Germany to seek a truce on the basis of the Fourteen Points. The Allies made clear that was a nonstarter. They compelled Germany to evacuate territory to the 1870 border, grant Allies bridgeheads across the Rhine, surrender its surface and submarine fleet, and turn over vast amounts of weapons.

Wilson shocked many Americans by announcing he would personally lead in the treaty negotiations at Versailles, France. His team included no leading Republicans. Wilson soon learned that his Allied counterparts had very different objectives from his Fourteen Points. He tolerated the disagreeable terms, placing faith in a new international organization, the League of Nations, to achieve a fair and lasting peace.

Upon his return, Wilson tried to rally support for the treaty, but the public was tired of war and international affairs. Republicans objected to various components and proposed changes to the treaty. Wilson, however, would not budge. While campaigning for the treaty, Wilson suffered a massive stroke. The Senate never ratified the Treaty of Versailles. Two years later, in 1921, the United States and Germany signed a separate peace agreement to end World War I.

More than 50,000 American troops were killed in action and 200,000 were wounded. Another 57,000 at home and abroad died of disease, totaling about 1 percent of the military fatalities on both sides in the war. The war cost the United States $32 billion.

After the war, the United States demobilized rapidly. The government terminated all materiel contracts immediately, leaving manufacturers to bear the cost of reconversion.

Military units on the Western Front returned home so quickly that by June 1919 only Pershing's headquarters and a small military contingent remained in Europe. Upon arriving home, troops received physical examinations, got paid back wages plus a small bonus, and went home with helmet, gas mask, and uniform.

The last troops to make it home were those sent to the newly established Soviet Union. When Russia collapsed and the Communists seized control of the country, Britain and France called for Allied intervention around Archangel in northwest Russia to secure supplies, aid Czechoslovakian troops who were serving on the Eastern Front, and eventually fight the Bolsheviks. Wilson sent some 5,000 Americans to join a British contingent. In the end, the Americans suffered 400 casualties for no real purpose and were withdrawn in mid-1919.

A second expedition went to Siberia on the Pacific Coast. Baker warned the American commander that he was undertaking a politically explosive campaign because of Japanese ambitions in the region. The Americans agreed to match the Japanese force of 7,000, but Japan sent 72,000. Communist successes and diplomatic pressure soured Japan's goal of holding some territory there. The United States evacuated in 1920; Japan left two years later. As *Literary Digest* concluded: "Some might have liked us if we had intervened less...some might have disliked us less if we had intervened more...but having concluded to intervene no more nor less than we actually did, nobody had any use for us at all."

Although some individuals proposed dramatic changes for the military, such as an independent air force or the abolition of the Marine Corps, Congress funded a relatively small military establishment without significant structural changes. In times of major wars, the United States would continue to rely on citizen soldier. Nevertheless, the size and scope of the war and introduction of new technology drove significant changes in each service.

Technology alone is not likely to transform warfare. It needs to fit into a kind of operational triangle with sound doctrine and organization to exploit its advantages properly. So it was with tanks and airplanes. Both weapons exhibited great promise, but three factors impeded their development: resistance to change within the military, a burgeoning peace movement, and a penurious Congress in the 1920s, followed by competing social demands during the Great Depression.

During World War I, the United States organized tanks into the Tank Corps and utilized them to overcome trench warfare. Despite their overall effectiveness, they moved slowly, roughly at the speed of infantrymen, and broke down frequently. After the war the Tank Corps was disbanded and the army struggled over where to place the vehicles. Many cavalrymen resisted mechanization, while others sought tanks that would continue to service infantry. Nor was there much funding in an era of tight budgets for the development of mechanized units. By the late 1930s, though, technology made mechanization more feasible, as did the vision of certain leaders. In 1940, the Army created the Armored Force to develop doctrine and oversee training and equipment under Maj. Gen. Adna Chaffee Jr., an advocate of mechanization. Chaffee died the next year, but he and others had broken down resistance and demonstrated the value of armored units and mechanized infantry in training maneuvers.

Airpower had the advantage of easy publicity after the fascination during the war. Most American aviators embraced the doctrine of strategic bombardment as a means of overcoming the brutality and losses of ground fighting. Aircraft that could drop bombs on factories and transportation systems and terrorize civilians would break morale at home and at the front, compelling opposing nations to surrender and saving vast numbers of lives.

When the Army cut back on aviation, Billy Mitchell led the charge for an independent air force and the development of a long-range bomber. He arranged for a publicized test of airpower, sinking several ships, including a captured German battleship, with bombs, which the Navy interpreted as a challenge to the battleship fleet. Mitchell continued to make waves on behalf of airpower, even from his new assignment in San Antonio. When two aviation disasters occurred, Mitchell released a memorandum to the press that placed blame on the "incompetency, criminal negligence, and almost treasonable administration of our National Defense by the Navy and War Departments." His court-martial for misconduct was a show trial in defense of airpower. He was found guilty and suspended without pay for five years. Mitchell resigned.

Over the next decade and a half, airmen worked largely within the system, eventually securing the production of the B-17 long-range bomber. With strategic bombing doctrine and a weapon, the airmen sought an independent air force. The army was not willing to go that far, but in 1939 George C. Marshall became chief of staff. He granted much greater independence to the Air Corps and its chief, Maj. Gen. Henry "Hap" Arnold.

Postwar poverty and a growing peace movement convinced governments to prevent a naval arms race. Just weeks after Mitchell's bombing exhibition, the Washington Naval Conference opened, bringing together world naval powers to limit warship tonnage, including new aircraft carriers, gun calibers, and naval fortifications. The agreement set 500,000-ton limits for the United States and Great Britain, 300,000 tons for Japan, and 175,000 tons for Italy and France. Signatories had to suspend the construction of new ships and decommission older ones.

Although the Joint Army-Navy Board investigated Mitchell's demonstration and decided that national security required greater development of aviation, it also stated that the battleship was the backbone of the fleet. Critics such as retired Admiral Sims hammered at the uniformed leaders who viewed carriers as a threat to Mahanian doctrine, when in fact they breathed some new life into it. In 1920 the United States built its first aircraft carrier, and in 1926, it converted two battle cruisers into carriers. Because the United States had so few and needed them in both the Atlantic and Pacific, the Navy built smaller carriers that fit through the Panama Canal.

During the interwar years the Marine Corps made the greatest headway. Reduced in size during demobilization, the marines maximized their limited resources and their quasi independence.

Led by Maj. Gen. John A. Lejeune, the commandant, marines discovered a vital mission: amphibious operations. They exploited their small size, created doctrine, and eventually found technology to achieve their mission.

The Joint Army-Navy Board had formulated war strategies against various countries. Called the Color Plans, the most likely one was Plan Orange (war with Japan). The plan required the seizure of Pacific islands by amphibious landings, and Lejeune focused the Marine Corps on it. He ordered Maj. Earl H. Ellis to investigate amphibious operations and offer creative solutions to problems. In Operation Plan 712, Ellis laid out the basis for amphibious warfare in World War II. They must land in waves, with heavy pre-landing bombardment by sea and air and a naval box barrage to protect the marines. He also saw the need for amphibious tanks, trucks, artillery, and other vehicles. Lejeune embraced the plan and emphasized amphibious operations at all levels of marine schooling. By 1938, the navy adopted the marines' amphibious landing manual. With organization and doctrine in hand, the marines acquired amphibious crafts by modifying civilian technology, providing them with tracked and untracked vehicles.

In the early 1930s, the international climate began changing. Japan invaded China in 1932, and the following year Adolf Hitler rose to power in Germany. Two years later, Benito Mussolini directed his Italian army to invade Ethiopia. In each instance, the international reaction was muted. The unparalleled violence in World War I and the hardships of the Great Depression left the world with little stomach for more bloodshed. In 1928, the United States joined 61 nations in signing the Kellogg-Briand Peace Pact, which outlawed war as a means of national policy. At home the Great Depression distracted attention from international affairs, and when Congress acted it was usually to avoid future confrontations. In the period 1934–35, a congressional committee headed by Rep. Gerald Nye investigated the munitions industry during World War I. The Nye Commission determined that corporations fomented war, bribed politicians, shared patents, divided business, and reaped enormous profits. In response, Congress passed a series of laws known collectively as the Neutrality Acts. Legislation placed an impartial embargo on arms sales, forbade loans to belligerents, and authorized the president to withhold passports of Americans traveling in war zones. President Franklin D. Roosevelt privately objected but he needed congressional support for domestic legislation, so he signed them.

While Congress and the American people were trying to distance themselves from world troubles, the military was not. By the late 1930s, a more progressive element had won the turf battles. Reductions in manpower and budget cuts had compelled the military to institute changes that emphasized the intellectual aspects of professionalism. With few command assignments and limited money for field training, branches placed greater emphasis on class rank in various post-graduate military schools. Workdays in peacetime were often short, leaving more time for professional reading, private war-gaming, and military analysis among motivated officers. Thus a number of officers developed as creative thinkers and problem solvers, comprehended the advantages of new technology, and adapted well to the changing nature of warfare.

Formalized planning took place on the initiative of military and political leaders. In the early 1930s, Chief of Staff Douglas MacArthur and his successor prepared manpower mobilization plans and began stockpiling weapons for national defense. A joint munitions board and the War Resources Agency gathered information and planned for industrial mobilization, but Roosevelt's aversion to superagencies hindered their efforts until 1943, when he authorized the creation of the Office of War Mobilization. In strategic planning, the Army-Navy Board discarded outdated Color Plans and formulated the Rainbow

Plans, which ranged from Continental defense to a multi-theater war in cooperation with allies (Rainbow #5).

It took war in Europe, however, for the United States to convert planning into action. In 1938, Germany overran Austria and Czechoslovakia. When Germany invaded Poland in 1939, France and Britain declared war. Congress allowed arms sales on a cash-and-carry basis, but not until Germany overran France in mid-1940 did the United States take sides. The United States agreed to trade old destroyers for British land bases and implemented its first peacetime draft. In March 1941 it created the lend-lease program, which purchased food, fuel, and equipment and gave them to America's allies. While lend-lease helped convert industry to a wartime footing, it slowed American military expansion by limiting supplies and equipment at home. Lend-lease eventually totaled 17 percent of U.S. military expenditures and helped feed and mechanize Allied armies.

Military leaders from the United States and Great Britain began to formulate plans. As a result of these meetings, the United States recognized Germany as the greatest threat and adopted a Europe-first approach. The navy began escorting supply convoys and firing on German ships and submarines on the high seas. In August 1941, Roosevelt and Prime Minister Winston Churchill joined the military staffs at a gathering in Newfoundland, where they agreed to postwar goals. The resulting Atlantic Charter called for self-determination of peoples, freer trade, greater disarmament, and an international organization to maintain peace.

During these meetings, Roosevelt told Churchill he would seek an incident to bring the United States into the war against Germany. He conceded that Congress hesitantly embraced preparedness, extending the term of 1940 draftees by one vote in the House of Representatives.

Nor was Germany the only aggressor nation. Japan had penetrated deeper into China, and after France fell it had launched an invasion of Southeast Asia. Congress responded by authorizing the president to restrict the exportation of material that was vital to national defense and later imposed an oil embargo on Japan.

With tensions mounting and its oil dwindling to a six-month supply, Japan decided to act. It planned a major thrust into the oil-rich Dutch East Indies to ensure a protected oil flow home. To implement its expansionist policy known as the Greater East Asia Co-Prosperity Sphere, Japan also planned an invasion of the Philippines and an attack on the U.S. Pacific fleet at Pearl Harbor. The Japanese had long resented U.S. domestic discriminatory policies toward Asians, and while Japanese leadership recognized the overwhelming industrial strength of the United States, it also believed Americans had no stomach for a tough, prolonged war.

On December 7, 1941, six Japanese aircraft carriers and some submarines slipped by sloppy American reconnaissance and attacked the U.S. fleet at anchor and its aircraft lined up wing-to-wing to protect against sabotage. Two hours later, 3,600 Americans were killed or wounded, 19 U.S. ships were sunk or disabled, and 292 planes were damaged or destroyed.
Both U.S. aircraft carriers were at sea and missed the attack. That day, Japan struck U.S. forces in the Philippines, followed by a major invasion two weeks later. Congress declared war on Japan on December 8, and three days later Germany declared war on the United States. Despite claims that Roosevelt knew of the attack in advance, evidence from MAGIC—a cryptanalysis program deciphering high-level Japanese military and diplomatic communications—proved that charge false.

In late 1941, the unemployment rate stood at close to 10 percent. Prewar planning assumed the United States could uniform approximately 15 million people before it hurt domestic production. In fact, over the course of sixty months, the war drew 16 million people into the armed forces through enlistment and a draft. One-third of a million were women.

Roosevelt set tremendous production goals for the nation. By the war's end, the United States had built more than 100 aircraft carriers, 1,500 naval vessels, 6,000 huge commercial ships, 300,000 aircraft, 630,000 jeeps, 88,000 tanks, 6.5 million rifles, 40 billion ammunition rounds, 434 million tons of steel, and 3 atomic bombs. Wartime mobilization and its economic reverberations created 17 million new jobs, plus 13 million more who served in uniform at peak.

Having emerged from the Great Depression, the public's mindset could not have been better. Only one-third of the gross national product (GNP) went to the war. Roosevelt hoped to maintain wartime support by providing goods and services at home. Production required improved skill levels, and as workers mastered them wages rose 68 percent, while the cost of living increased 23 percent. People had jobs and consumed extravagantly. Prices were frozen, but many folks had to work overtime, which gave them additional spending money.

The United States financed 45 percent of its war effort through taxation, twice the rate of World War I. The remainder it raised through bond sales. The government tapped the massive outpouring of patriotism after Pearl Harbor. Those who could not serve could contribute by working and purchasing war bonds.

Wartime demands altered the United States dramatically. Rural folks rushed to the cities, where jobs were plentiful, leaving farm communities with labor shortages. More than 6 million women entered the workplace, as did millions of Blacks who migrated northward. Businesses hired Blacks last, but in time many learned valuable skills for the postwar world. California became a boom state. Rather than ship manufacture war materials across the country, they began building them on the West Coast. California's population increased by 2 million during the war, taxing local supplies and creating shantytowns for the employed.

African Americans were not the only ones to suffer discrimination. The United States targeted persons of Japanese ancestry as disloyal. Californians had discriminated against Japanese for decades, and officials now gathered 127,000 Japanese Americans and placed them in relocation centers. Incarcerated families lost generations of accumulated wealth, selling their property for mere pennies on the dollar. Individuals who were loyal to the United States endured the indignity of living within barbed-wire enclosure camps. In 1944, the U.S. Supreme Court declared the policy constitutional.

By late 1941, the Allied war effort had stabilized at a low level. The German surprise offensive stalled just outside Moscow. The only aid the United States could provide the Soviets at the time was through lend-lease. Great Britain stoutly resisted German air attacks, ensuring that an invasion of the British Isles could not succeed. Still, Germany and Italy occupied most of Europe and a large portion of North Africa.

In planning operations, the United States balanced the needs of two theaters, interservice rivalries, finite resources, and the interests and demands of its allies. In the European Theater, the army played the dominant role and largely dictated military strategy and operations; the navy's principal role was controlling the sea lanes, transporting troops and supplies overseas, and planning and supporting amphibious landings. In the vast Pacific Theater, there was a greater balance between the army and the navy.

Drawing on lessons from World War I, Marshall created three superstructures—Army Ground Forces (doctrine and training), Army Service Forces (logistics), and Army Air Forces (airpower)—

while he worked mostly with Operations Division (OPD), which oversaw operations and plans. It was there that Dwight D. Eisenhower emerged as Marshall's right-hand man. A former assistant to MacArthur, Eisenhower came to Marshall as a Pacific Theater expert, but his strategic and operational thinking, good judgment, and capacity to make sound decisions elevated him to the head of OPD.

Marshall and Eisenhower believed they would ultimately have to defeat Germany in continental Europe, requiring an invasion across the English Channel. Unfortunately, the British hesitated. Americans had faith in the mobility and striking power of armies with improvements in aircraft, tanks, and other vehicles; the British worried that armies would bog down as in World War I and sustain catastrophic losses. Instead, the British argued for operations in North Africa, where they had gained some momentum and where American forces could acquire some combat experience. It would also take a few years to train and build up Allied strength for a successful cross-channel invasion. Although Marshall and others were shocked by this peripheral approach, Roosevelt overrode his subordinates and ordered American participation. The American public clamored for fighting and they had to keep the coalition together.

For future planning, the Americans created the Joint Chiefs of Staff (JCS), with the Army, Navy, Army Air Corps, and eventually Marine Corps as representatives to plan strategy and advise Roosevelt. The president designated Adm. William D. Leahy as its chairman. They, along with selected civilian advisers, met with their British counterparts as Combined Chiefs of Staff (CCS).

In the Pacific arena, coalition warfare was not quite so integrated. The British and Chinese largely directed strategy and operations on mainland Asia, much to the frustration of U.S. generals Joseph Stillwell and Claire Chennault. Since the United States, with aid from Australia and New Zealand, would execute most of the operations elsewhere in the Pacific, the United States dictated strategy and operations. MacArthur oversaw the war in the Southwest Pacific and Adm. Chester W. Nimitz headed the Central Pacific.

In the North African campaign, the Allies hoped to enlist French support and open the Mediterranean Sea for shipping. Because the United States would contribute a majority of the troops, Eisenhower was chosen to oversee the campaign. The plan called for a giant pincer movement: the British to advance westward toward Tunisia, while the Americans, after winning over French support, and other British troops pushing eastward. In November 1942, a massive landing with 400 ships, 1,000 aircraft, and 107,000 troops took place. As the British advanced from the south, Eisenhower closed in from the west and halted along some high ground in west Tunisia, giving the German commander, Field Marshall Erwin Rommel, a chance to attack. He planned to break through the American line, seize the Allies' supply base, and drive on to the coast, trapping the Allies. The American commander Maj. Gen. Lloyd Fredendall dispersed his tanks and commandeered the engineering assets for his headquarters. The Germans crashed through the weak American lines at Kasserine Pass, but fortune soon shifted against them when the German forces advanced on a route that British troops held. The timely arrival of four American battalions of heavy artillery enabled the Allies to check the breakthrough. The Germans then withdrew.

The Americans suffered 5,300 losses at Kasserine Pass. Almost as important, it took a year for the British leaders to shake their distrust of American soldiers, and they were convinced that they needed to "shape" Eisenhower's decisions and minimize his involvement in planning and operations.

Maj. Gen. George S. Patton replaced Fredendall as commander of II Corps. He immediately rejuvenated morale and launched an attack from the south, eventually linking with the British. By

April, Patton was removed to plan for the invasion of Sicily and Maj. Gen. Omar Bradley took over II Corps. Some Germans and Italians escaped the Allied noose, but in May 1943, 275,000 troops surrendered in North Africa.

With the momentum on their side, the Allies agreed over the objections of the American generals to invade Sicily and then Italy. In July 1943, the Allies landed in Sicily, as gale winds and strong enemy resistance proved nearly disastrous for the U.S. forces. Once ashore, the plan was for the Americans to block the Germans on the west while the British drove on to Messina. Instead, the British advanced slowly due to heavy resistance and the Americans broke out, slicing the island and seizing Palermo and then Messina. The American forces, aided by the Sherman tank and other improved equipment, exhibited aggressiveness and extraordinary mobility amid the difficult terrain. The Allies lost 22,000 troops, compared to 100,000 Italian soldiers, most of whom surrendered, and 10,000 Germans.

Although Italy surrendered on the eve of the invasion, the Allies proceeded with their plans to lock down substantial German troops and to secure airfields to bomb Germany. In early September, British forces landed at the toe and the arch of the Italian "boot" against modest opposition. The Americans encountered stiff resistance, and Naples, a valuable port, did not fall until early October. The Allies then bogged down well south of Rome, which finally fell in June 1944. Still, the Germans resisted fiercely as the Allies ground out their advances. Not until May 1945 did the Germans in Italy surrender.

The Italian Campaign played a vital role in the war. Despite the Allies fighting with limited resources, Germany committed 26 divisions to Italy. The theater also provided valuable airfields for bombing Germany.

To launch a cross-channel invasion, the Allies had to stockpile troops, weapons, and supplies, and this required control of the seas. Early war losses to German submarines were staggering. Through June 1942, Allied losses had exceeded shipbuilding by 2.8 million tons. The Allies used convoys in conjunction with air patrols. German submarines hunted in packs. Allies intercepted their regular communications through direction-finding radio equipment and ULTRA, the ability to decode German communications, to determine their location and plans, helping to turn the tide in the Battle of the Atlantic. In the last two years of the war, the Allies reduced supply ship losses by 85 percent.

In Europe, the Allies possessed four advantages that were vital to their success. First, although the Germans had better tanks and weapons, the Allies had superior artillery and aircraft, and their tanks and vehicles were simple in design, durable, quick to build, easy to repair, fast, and mobile. Second, ULTRA enabled the Allies to plan and execute major operations more effectively. Third, with the modified P-51 fighter plane, the British and American air forces gained control of the skies, protecting bombers and assisting Allied ground troops. Fourth, they had the Soviet Union as allies. By June 1944, the Soviets had killed 2 million German soldiers and compelled Germany to commit 165 divisions there, leaving 59 in France and the Low Countries. Those factors, along with ingenuity and some hard fighting and service, enabled them to defeat the Germans.

At dawn on June 6, 1944, five Allied divisions plus airborne troops landed successfully in Normandy, despite heavy resistance, especially at Omaha Beach. Over the next seven weeks, the Americans seized the Contentin Peninsula, but the Allies made limited progress elsewhere, as the *bocage* (dense hedgerows) that enclosed agricultural fields limited fighting to the roads.

By late July, Americans managed to restore mobility. A coordinated tactical air and ground attack broke through the weakened

German lines. Patton's Third Army passed to the front, mopping up German resistance to the west and then pivoting eastward to encircle the enemy. Hitler refused to authorize a retreat and even ordered a counterattack, which worked to Allied advantage. Yet Bradley, now commanding the 12th Army Group, failed to close the loop and the backbone of the German army in France escaped.

In August 1944, Paris fell to the Allies, and it appeared as though the war might end that year. Germany had suffered staggering losses, but as the Allies advanced deeper into France, severe supply problems emerged. Too little port space and too many troops, vehicles, and refugees slowed the advance, giving the Germans a chance to regroup. In mid-September, British Field Marshal Bernard Montgomery attempted a single thrust across Rhine into Germany. It failed.

The slow Allied advance gave the Germans time to resupply and accumulate forces for a major offensive. Hitler planned to strike the American troops in the Ardennes and drive to the northwest, seizing Antwerp and cutting off the Americans and British. He then hoped to negotiate a peace and concentrate on the Soviets. The surprise attack shattered several U.S. divisions and damaged others, yet pockets of American troops held critical crossroads long enough for reinforcements to arrive. African American troops voluntarily waived rank to serve in depleted White infantry units. These efforts enabled the Allies to regroup and launch a powerful counterattack that by late January hammered back the Germans. In the Battle of the Bulge, Americans suffered 75,000 casualties while the German army lost approximately 100,000.

With oil from various ports pouring into the Allied armies, mobility returned in March 1945. American infantrymen climbed on tanks and rode them through the countryside, disembarking when they encountered resistance. The Allies crossed the Rhine, encircled the Ruhr Valley, and roared through portions of Germany.

From the east, the Soviets drove deep into Germany, and resistance began to crumble. On April 30, 1945, Hitler committed suicide, and a week later Germany surrendered. The war in Europe was over, at a cost of 183,000 American lives.

Once Japan neutralized most of the Pacific Fleet, it focused on the Philippines. On December 22, 1941, Japan landed two divisions with naval and air support, compelling MacArthur to retreat to the Bataan Peninsula. In March, Roosevelt ordered MacArthur to Australia. Lt. Gen. Jonathan Wainwright and some troops resisted until May, when starvation forced their surrender. Many captives then perished on the brutal Bataan Death March or in prison camps.

The Japanese had secured an inner ring of defenses. Flush with victory, they hoped to build an outer ring that would break the American will to fight. Japan attempted to secure Port Moresby on the southern coast of New Guinea, from which it could bomb northern Australia. It also planned to destroy the two American carriers that were at sea during the attack at Pearl Harbor by landing forces in the Aleutian Islands, Alaska, drawing the U.S. carriers northward, and seizing Midway Island in their rear, trapping the carriers between a carrier task force and land-based aircraft. Fortunately for the Americans, MAGIC detected both plans.

In May 1942, in the Battle of the Coral Sea, the two American carriers and various other ships blocked the Japanese thrust around New Guinea. One American carrier was sunk and the USS *Yorktown* sustained bad damage, but they inflicted heavy aircraft and pilot loss and damaged an enemy carrier, forcing the Japanese to scuttle their operation.

At Midway, the Japanese sent a task force of four carriers and other ships; against this, Adm. Chester W. Nimitz had three carriers. The U.S. fleet avoided the Japanese submarine net and caught them by surprise. U.S. torpedo-bombers and then dive-bombers caught the Japanese with aircraft on deck loaded with bombs. Four Japanese carriers went down that day, along with 330 planes. The United States lost the repaired *Yorktown* and 150 aircraft. The victory neutralized the Japanese advantage, and despite the "Germany First" strategy, Chief of Naval Operations Ernest J. King and Marshall pushed to follow up the success with land attacks on Guadalcanal and New Guinea. Marines stormed ashore at Guadalcanal in August, aided by the army in October, and major fighting took place in the air, at sea, and on land. At Buna in New Guinea, the 32nd Division, ill equipped and untrained in jungle fighting, suffered over 90 percent casualties but won with help from Australians and American reinforcements. By February 1943, Allied forces secured both places.

That summer, the Americans decided to pursue two approaches to converge on Formosa: one along a Southwest Pacific (SWPA) route, directed by MacArthur, and another through the Central Pacific (CENPAC), commanded by Nimitz. MacArthur's "hit 'em where they ain't" approach limited losses and enabled Americans to bypass enemy strongholds, trapping Japanese forces on islands or in jungles. Nimitz's command also employed an island-hopping approach. CENPAC battled its way through the Gilbert and Marshall Islands, with the Marianas—Guam, Saipan, and Tinian—as its target. From there, the United States could launch bombing strikes on Japan.

Both areas benefited from new aircraft, naval vessels, and amphibious crafts that enhanced speed, firepower, and mobility. American industry built 24 new Essex-class carriers, which traveled at almost 35 knots and hauled 90 to 110 aircraft, along with dozens of smaller-class carriers. In the air, new torpedo-bombers, fighters, and dive-bombers gave the navy a significant technological advantage. American submarines sank so many Japanese supply ships and oil tankers that Japanese pilots

7. The 165th Infantry approaches Butaritari, Yellow Beach Two during the Battle of Makin in November 1943. Their attack, part of the island-hopping strategy of the Pacific Campaign, was slowed by coral bottom waters and Japanese machine-gun fire.

received only a few hours of training. American forces showcased skill, speed, and firepower in June 1944, in what was dubbed the "Marianas Turkey Shoot." American pilots shot down 346 Japanese planes at a cost of fewer than 30. Along with two Japanese carriers sunk by U.S. submarines and another by planes at long range, Japan lost 480 aircraft.

The United States had refined its amphibious practices and executed some extraordinary feats. By late 1943, more amphibious tanks and tracked vehicles arrived, which enhanced the speed and strength of landings. At Saipan in mid-June 1944, Lt. Gen. Holland Smith landed 8,000 marines in twenty minutes and nearly 20,000 by nightfall. By mid-August, Saipan, Guam, and

Tinian were in U.S. possession and bombers launched B-29 raids against Japan.

With the accelerated progress in both SWPA and CENPAC, the JCS decided to skip Formosa and have Nimitz go directly to Iwo Jima and Okinawa, while MacArthur liberated the Philippines. In October 1944, MacArthur launched an invasion of Leyte. The Japanese tried to lure the U.S. Navy into leaving the landing inadequately protected while another task force destroyed it. In the largest naval engagement in history, Adm. William Halsey chased the bait and sank four carriers. Meanwhile, the remaining American ships and aircraft bluffed the Japanese into retreating. Despite vigorous resistance, MacArthur's forces then defeated the Japanese at Leyte, Mindoro, and Luzon. Filipinos fought alongside Americans, and casualties on both sides were high.

Slow progress in the Philippines delayed the attack, but on February 19, 1945, the United States landed at Iwo Jima, an eight-square-mile island filled with an extensive cave network. For more than one month, Marines battled Japanese forces, losing 6,821 men and suffering 25,000 casualties. With Iwo Jima in American hands, bombers could fly largely undetected until they approached the Japanese homeland.

At Okinawa, the Japanese had 100,000 troops plus artillery, fortifications, and caves. In April 1945, the United States launched its attack, eventually committing three marine and five army divisions. In addition, the United States assembled a massive armada including 40 large and small carriers, 18 battleships, and 200 destroyers. The Japanese resisted in depth, sustaining 100,000 losses, while inflicting 40,000 casualties. Japanese kamikaze (suicide) attacks were costly, too, killing 5,000 sailors and damaging or sinking 7 carriers and 325 total ships. Civilian losses at Okinawa totaled 100,000.

Strategic bombing doctrine argued that long-range bombers could destroy industry and crush the morale of the civilian population. In Europe, the British generally saturated cities with bombs in nighttime raids, as retaliation for terror bombing and to reduce losses. The United States incurred staggering losses in daylight bombing in B-17s. The Americans also hopped from one type of target to another, never really concentrating on a critical element of German production. The introduction of the P-51 fighter and the opening of a bombing front in Italy marked a dramatic shift. By D-Day, the Allies controlled the skies. German production shifted below ground, draining valuable resources, and 70 percent of all tonnage against Germany fell in the last ten months of the war. Although Allied bombing did not live up to prewar claims, it opened an extremely valuable front and utilized Allied strength more optimally.

The United States had long hoped to create another front against Japan from China, but it never quite developed. Americans got caught in a power struggle between the Nationalist leader Chiang Kai-shek and the Communist leader Mao Zedong. American pilots and ground forces never secured the bombing fields against Japan or manpower diversion that the Allies sought.

The fall of the Marianas enabled the United States to stage a strategic bombing campaign against Japan with B-29s. Confronted with bad weather, headwinds, and technical problems, the United States struggled until Maj. Gen. Curtis LeMay took charge. LeMay employed nighttime firebombing. In March 1945, one firebombing raid on Tokyo in high winds killed 84,000 and torched almost 16 square miles.

Despite massive destruction, the air war in both theaters highlighted a flaw in the strategic bombing doctrine. Conventional bombings did not break civilian will, nor did strategic bombing advocates anticipate that enemy leaders would refuse to respond to the plight of their people.

Work on the atomic bomb was begun by the Americans and the British before the Pearl Harbor attack. The Allies intended to use it against Germany and Japan. Roosevelt died on April 12, 1945, and shortly afterward new president Harry S. Truman learned of work on the bomb. In July 1945, the United States successfully exploded the first atomic weapon. Around the same time, the Allies issued the Potsdam Declaration, calling for the unconditional surrender of Japan but assuring its people of fair postwar treatment.

Multiple factors weighed on Truman in his decision to use the bomb. Heavy casualties at Okinawa predicted staggering losses for an invasion of Kyushu and the main island of Honshu. Neither economic blockade nor conventional strategic bombing had brought Japan to its knees, and the JCS viewed the atomic bombs as the best means of ending the war. Countervailing arguments from some scientists expressed moral qualms or called for a demonstration. Foreign-policy experts warned of postwar complications with the Soviet Union over using the bomb.

In the end, Truman considered the options and elected to use the bombs, primarily to save American lives and end the war as soon as possible. The United States decided to drop two bombs to convey the message that it had unlimited bombs, although it did not. On August 6, 1945, a B-29 exploded a device on Hiroshima, killing 60,000 people, giving radiation poisoning to another 60,000, and destroying 81 percent of the buildings. With no surrender forthcoming despite a Soviet declaration of war against Japan, the United States dropped a different atomic bomb on Nagasaki, killing 35,000, inflicting radiation poisoning on 40,000, and destroying half the buildings. Still, Japanese leaders remained steadfast until the emperor intervened. World War II was over.

The Allies won the war because they built and sustained an effective alliance. The United States military learned that traditional approaches failed under the weight of mobilization and warfare like that of the two world wars. It needed centralized organization and power to convert its superior resources and to focus those resources on the enemy. Just as technological innovation offered the military more weapons and equipment, so its officer corps had to conceptualize innovative plans to exploit the technological changes. They discarded old ways and applied new approaches to warfare.

The United States lost 416,000 in the armed forces and 2,000 more civilians, and more than 671,000 were wounded. It cost the country $304 billion. Worldwide, approximately 60 million people lost their lives in the war: 15 million battle deaths, 45 million civilian fatalities, and another 25 million wounded. The destruction, however, extended beyond the loss of life. The United States was a rarity. It did not suffer massive devastation. It would take years, sometimes decades, for countries to recover. And from the ashes of World War II emerged two victorious superpowers, the United States and the Soviet Union, allies once, but not for long.

Chapter 4
The limits of power

The United States emerged from World War II as the strongest nation in the world. Its booming economy was essentially untouched by the violence, and it boasted an experienced military with a monopoly on atomic weapons.

Over the next three decades, the United States promoted its vision of the Atlantic Charter, hoping to transform the world into its own image. Painfully, the United States learned that its economic and military power were finite, and since the 1970s it has struggled to absorb that lesson.

Before the war Marshall had the army create a manual on military government, and in April 1942 he established a school to train occupation troops. With the collapse of Germany, occupation troops removed Nazi officials and assumed greater responsibility for refugees, displaced persons, identifying and burying the dead, and administering services to the defeated population. In 1949, Britain, France, and the United States merged their occupation zones to form the Federal Republic of Germany; the fourth zone, overseen by the Soviet Union, became the German Democratic Republic (East Germany).

In Japan, the United States led Allied occupiers, with MacArthur placed in charge. To ensure a peaceful transition, the United

States permitted Japan to retain its emperor. By 1952, the Allies turned over authority for rule in Japan to a civilian government.

When Japan surrendered, the United States had 12 million people on active duty. The public clamored for them to return home. Fortunately, the military had planned demobilization carefully. Although the most experienced personnel rotated home first, it was the fairest system they could devise. By mid-1946, only 1.5 million remained, still a frustrating demobilization pace. As one soldier wrote his congressman, "You put us in the Army and you can get us out. Either demobilize us or, when given the next shot at the ballot box, we will demobilize you."

The war had pulled the United States out of the Great Depression, and many people feared a relapse when the war ended. To avoid a flood of returning veterans in search of jobs, the government passed the G.I. Bill, which offered them benefits such as free college tuition, a livable stipend for schooling, and low-interest home and business loans. The legislation eased the transition to a peacetime economy and offered opportunities for millions who otherwise would never have them, laying the groundwork for economic mobility.

Neither the Truman administration nor the military had any intention of reverting to the late 1930s conditions in size or structure. The administration wanted a military strength of 1.5 million, and the draft expired in 1947. To fill the dwindling ranks, Congress instituted a peacetime draft in 1948. The policy marked a dramatic shift from a military that depended on mobilizing citizen soldier to one that focused on readiness to deploy.

The war highlighted some serious weaknesses in the defense establishment that Congress tried to rectify with the National Security Act of 1947. Various intelligence-gathering elements failed to share information prior to Pearl Harbor, and the legislation established the Central Intelligence Agency (CIA) to oversee the collection, analysis, and dissemination of intelligence. For nearly three decades, the Army aviators lobbied for independence, and their contributions in World War II, along with reliance on the atomic bomb for defense, ensured the creation of an independent air force.

World War II demonstrated the complexity of warfare and the need for greater inter-service cooperation. The Joint Chiefs of Staff (JCS) had secured collaboration in planning, but battles such as Leyte Gulf indicated the need for better joint operations. The 1947 legislation made the JCS permanent and created a National Military Establishment under a secretary of defense to improve joint planning and operations. Finally, the law created the National Security Council, which brought together the central players of national defense and security, such as the president, the JCS, the secretary of defense, the CIA director, the secretary of state, a national security adviser, and various cabinet members as needed. The legislation marked a dramatic shift of power in peacetime away from the State Department and to the military and national security sphere. It also paved the way for new joint-military schools, such as the National War College, and think tanks that brought in civilian experts to advise and solve problems.

Unfortunately, the National Security Act of 1947 was flawed. The Air Force and Navy vied for funding for atomic weapons-delivery systems and a greater share of the budget. Service secretaries (secretaries of the army, navy, and air force) retained too much authority and skirted the secretary of defense to lobby Congress for more resources. When the secretary of defense chose seventy air force bomber groups over a navy supercarrier, current and retired admirals publicly challenged the decision. Omar Bradley, chairman of the JCS, branded their conduct as "open rebellion against civilian control." Congress ultimately backed the secretary's decision and passed an amendment in 1949 that created the Department of Defense (DOD), with the secretary of defense as its head. The various service secretaries and the JCS reported to the secretary of defense.

The other major change was the integration of the armed forces. African Americans had fought in every major war other than the Mexican-American War. Since the Civil War, they had served in separate units except on ships, where they were relegated to menial duties. In World War II, Black soldiers fought in two infantry divisions, flew boldly as Tuskegee airmen, earned officer ranks in the Navy, shattered the color barrier in the Marine Corps, hauled oil and supplies across Europe in the Red Ball Express, and even waived rank and fought as privates in White regiments at the Battle of the Bulge. In recognition of their invaluable service, Truman announced that the armed forces would integrate. African Americans rejoiced over the decision, and despite numerous bumps, the armed services soon became the most integrated element in society.

The United States and Russia had never been particularly close, and when the communist Soviet Union emerged from World War I, relations worsened. As allies in World War II, both sides hoped for good relations in the postwar years. Roosevelt tried to present the brutal Stalin in a positive light, and the Soviets played up the idea of Americans as allies.

Unfortunately, three critical wartime and postwar events soured the relationship. The Soviets bore the brunt of the German onslaught and desperately wanted a second front in northern Europe, which did not happen until mid-1944. Soviet military deaths amounted to nearly ten times those of the United States, and Stalin was suspicious of Allied motives. The Soviets publicly derided lend-lease, even though it comprised one-sixth of the Soviet military's GNP and Stalin admitted privately that it was invaluable. The second clash was over postwar loans. The Soviets badly needed loans to rebuild, and the United States tried to leverage them for free trade and self-determination of Eastern

Europe. The third problem revolved around self-determination of peoples. The United States and Great Britain pledged that principle in the Atlantic Charter, which the Soviets never endorsed. Stalin had promised a free election in Poland, but when the time came he concluded that a freely elected Polish government would be unfriendly to the Soviet Union, which had suffered two invasions through weak western neighbors over twenty-seven years. Roosevelt seemed to understand this but failed to warn the American public. With a heavy Polish-American population, Truman viewed Poland as a test case for Soviet postwar conduct and interpreted it as Soviet duplicity.

Fundamentally, the two parties clashed over ideology, intentions, and leadership. While communist ideology called for its spread worldwide, Stalin sought its expansion as a means of protecting the Soviet Union. Shortly after the war, it created a string of Eastern European satellites. By contrast, the United States believed in free people, free trade, and capitalism.

Neither Truman nor Stalin trusted the other. In a speech in the Senate in 1941, Truman suggested that the United States aid the Soviets or the Germans, whichever side was losing, in hopes they would kill each other off. He viewed the Soviets as two-faced and unconcerned with other peoples. Stalin perceived Truman as one-sided and incorrigible. After the tremendous losses in World War II, Stalin believed Soviet security superseded the right of Eastern Europeans to choose their own leaders. He considered U.S. proposals, such as the offer to turn over its atomic bombs and atomic secrets to the United Nations (UN) after every country underwent inspection, a means of preserving the military imbalance.

To block Soviet expansion, the United States adopted a strategy of containment. George F. Kennan, a Soviet expert in the State Department, first articulated it in a lengthy telegram in 1946, followed two years later by an anonymous article under the byline

"X" in *Foreign Affairs*. Kennan argued that the USSR had such severe internal problems and dissension that it must continue to expand to endure. If the United States and its allies could prevent expansion, internal strife would ultimately lead to its dissolution. Although the United States did not adopt containment officially until National Security Council Report 68 (NSC-68) in 1950, it did take steps to check communist expansion in 1947 when Truman issued the Truman Doctrine, which declared that the United States must assist free people from subjugation by minorities or external elements. That same year the United States created the Marshall Plan, a $12 billion aid program to help buoy the Western European economy and prevent it from falling to communism by sending U.S.-made goods and equipment to its allies. The Soviets, unwilling to divulge economic information, declined to participate.

Truman feared the American people would lapse into their 1930s isolationist ways, and he kept them engaged and preserved congressional support by playing up the Red Scare, fear of a communist takeover around the world. In 1949, the fall of mainland China to communism (now People's Republic of China, or PRC) and the Soviet explosion of its first atomic device seemed to confirm Truman's fears. The United States responded by organizing the North Atlantic Treaty Organization (NATO) and signing other collective-security agreements around the world to check communist expansion.

At the end of World War II, the United States and Soviet Union jointly occupied the Korean peninsula, creating North and South Korea. Both Koreas sought unification on their own terms. After North Korea sponsored a failed insurgency, it decided to resort to conventional weapons with support from the PRC and the USSR.

The door opened in 1950 when Secretary of State Dean Acheson delivered a speech that designated a U.S. defense line through Japan and the Philippines. North Korea interpreted that to mean the United States would not protect South Korea. In June 1950, Soviet-made tanks and North Korean troops crossed the border, crashing through the South Korean Army (ROK). With Washington's consent, MacArthur deployed understrength troops as a stopgap measure; North Korean forces overwhelmed them. Aid came from U.S.-based bombers and reinforcements rushed over from Japan. Lt. Gen. Walton H. Walker was then able to stabilize the defense in the southeast corner of South Korea called the Pusan Perimeter.

Truman took the issue of the invasion to the UN Security Council for intervention. Fortunately, the USSR was boycotting the UN for designating Nationalist China, not the PRC, for the Chinese seat. The Security Council demanded a ceasefire and then called on its member nations to defend South Korea. Fifteen countries sent troops and six others provided medical assistance in a war largely run by the United States. MacArthur was placed in charge.

To strengthen the forces, Truman recalled several National Guard divisions and reserves from World War II, much to their disgruntlement. Most felt they had already done their duty in World War II and that others should shoulder the burden. The UN quickly built a massive force at Pusan, soon outnumbering the North Koreans.

MacArthur planned to conduct an amphibious landing at Inchon and retake Seoul, while Walker attacked along the Pusan Perimeter. MacArthur designated the X Corps (a marine and an army division) to make the mid-September landing. Despite serious doubts from the JCS, MacArthur won their support, and the landing was a fantastic success. To the south, Walker encountered some initial resistance but soon drove back the North Koreans.

Having gained momentum, MacArthur requested and received approval to cross the 38th Parallel into North Korea. Some officials worried about Chinese intervention, but MacArthur and others dismissed it. Then, MacArthur got careless. He withdrew the X Corps for an unnecessary landing on the Pacific coast, stretching thin the troops above the 38th Parallel and creating gaps between various commands amid difficult terrain.

MacArthur ignored several warnings that China would enter the conflict. As cold weather set in, troops reached the Yalu River, the border between the PRC and North Korea. First a trickle and then a deluge of Chinese soldiers attacked. Caught outnumbered and dispersed, the UN forces fell back. Some, like the marines at Chosin Reservoir, endured horrific conditions to escape. Although the UN command had suffered heavy losses, it managed to regroup around the 38th Parallel. When Walker died in a jeep accident, the acclaimed World War II airborne officer Matthew Ridgway replaced him.

Ridgway turned the forces around and seized the initiative, relying on increased firepower to compensate for Chinese numbers. When the Chinese launched their counterattack, the UN forces responded with night attacks to prevent the Chinese from fortifying their positions and employing "fight and roll," exacting a heavy price on attackers and then retreating to another prepared position.

MacArthur was stunned by the Chinese success, and he called for an invasion of mainland China. Republicans also wanted the war expanded, while Truman and the JCS hoped to keep it limited. Unfortunately, MacArthur had cultivated strong ties with the Republicans in Congress. Truman gently criticized him for his cozy arrangement and had warned him about announcing policies without consent of the White House. When Soviet-made MiG-15s began shooting down U.S. bombers, the JCS prohibited bombing airfields in China and instead rushed F-86s to Korea to restore air superiority. MacArthur chafed. Then he laid out terms for an armistice without clearing them with U.S. officials. The last straw

8. In one of the greatest feats in U.S. military history, Marines in the First Division endured bitter-cold weather at Chosin Reservoir, Korea, in December 1950, while fighting their way to safety against tremendous numbers of Chinese attackers.

was when he wrote a letter to the House minority leader in March 1951 that was made public, calling for an enlarged war. As Chairman Bradley testified, it was "the wrong war at the wrong place at the wrong time." With the full support of the JCS and Secretary of Defense George C. Marshall, Truman removed MacArthur and installed Ridgway as UN commander. Congress ultimately held hearings, which went nowhere.

Ridgway's troops continued their drive against the North Koreans and Chinese until they reached an effective tactical position near the 38th Parallel, where UN forces halted in June 1951. The idea of a unified Korea was militarily unachievable without widening the war. For nearly two more years, both sides battled over the same terrain. When Stalin died in March 1953, the new Soviet leadership was no longer willing to provide the Chinese with weapons and equipment. The new U.S. president, Eisenhower, also wanted the war ended. On July 27, 1953, the two sides signed an armistice, exchanging prisoners who wanted to return to their homeland and creating a demilitarized zone approximating the 38th Parallel.

The United States had more than 36,000 killed with 7,800 missing. More than 100,000 Americans sustained wounds. Estimated losses for the Chinese and North Koreans are 1 million dead plus 600,000 civilian deaths. South Korea suffered 217,000 troops killed and about 1 million civilian deaths. The war cost the United States $67 billion. The United States has stationed troops in South Korea ever since.

Truman used the Korean War and the Red Scare to spur Congress to increase defense spending despite a great deficit. By June 1951, with 3.6 million in uniform, costs escalated from $52.4 billion in fiscal year 1947 (FY47) to $442.3 billion in FY53. Eisenhower believed the economy was the backbone of U.S. power, and he wanted to rein in military spending before it affected domestic growth. His solution was the New Look.

Eisenhower realized that manpower was very expensive and that the Soviets would badly outnumber NATO in Western Europe. Nuclear weapons, by contrast, were comparatively cheap. He decided to cut back on personnel and place his resources in a nuclear basket. From 1954 to 1960, he reduced manpower strength 25 percent and cut the budget by 22 percent. Only the price of the delivery systems—air force and navy bombers and work on ballistic and intercontinental ballistic missiles (ICBMs) from aircraft, land, ships, and submarines—kept the cuts from being deeper.

Money and research ultimately led Eisenhower to warn the American public of the military-industrial complex: companies reaped great profits from military production, stirred fears to boost military spending, and convinced politicians to buy unnecessary weapons. Since colonial America, those who provided services for the military reaped great profits, but the money and stakes were not as great as in the 1950s.

In addition to promoting an expansion of the feared military-industrial complex, Eisenhower's New Look limited options to massive retaliation. If communists acted aggressively, the United States could respond only with the threat or actual use of nuclear weapons, in what Secretary of State John Foster Dulles called "brinksmanship." Those limited options handcuffed American foreign policy and generated frustration, particularly in the army and the Marine Corps, whose role shrank. The military set up a tripwire system of tactical and strategic nuclear weapons to deter an invasion of Western Europe. Experts began formulating nuclear strategies that would enable the United States to survive war, or so they believed. Both the United States and Soviet Union stockpiled nuclear weapons, more than enough to blow up the world many times over. Eisenhower relied on that nuclear deterrence, American scientific and technological innovation, and economic strength to shield the United States and its allies.

For the first time in the nation's history in peacetime, the public worried that the United States and the world as they knew it might be different the next morning. Schoolchildren practiced absurd drills to survive nuclear attack, which only served to scare them and their parents. Families stockpiled canned goods in case of nuclear war; some even built underground bunkers to survive a nuclear holocaust.

The greatest nuclear crisis occurred in October 1962, when aerial reconnaissance photographs indicated the Soviets were constructing missile silos for their medium- and intermediate-range nuclear missiles in Cuba. President John F. Kennedy ordered a naval quarantine of Cuba, demanded the Soviets remove the missiles and warheads, and alerted the American public on television of the crisis. The Democratic Party leadership had a reputation of being soft on communism—Eastern Europe and China had fallen to communism during Truman's watch, and Kennedy authorized the CIA to attempt a disastrous invasion by Cuban exiles at the Bay of Pigs—and Kennedy felt he had to make a strong stand. With the United States on military readiness and tensions extremely high, the Soviet Union vowed to remove the silos and nuclear weapons; the United States agreed not to invade Cuba and would remove the outdated missiles in Turkey soon. Both sides backed away from nuclear war and a year later implemented a nuclear test ban.

Although the American public believed the United States was far behind the Soviets in nuclear missiles, in 1960 the United States had 18,000 nuclear weapons. By the late 1960s, the United States relied on the "triad" of nuclear bombers, nuclear land-based missiles (1,054), and nuclear missiles fired from submarines (656). With so many nuclear weapons on both sides, deterrence rested with mutually assured destruction (MAD). By 1970, the United States developed the first multiple independent re-entry vehicle (MIRV), numerous warheads on an ICBM that were programmed to strike separate targets, making it much more difficult for any antiballistic missile defense system to succeed. The Soviets followed suit, compensating for accuracy with larger warheads.

As the nuclear arms race soared, the two nations sought to inject a bit of sanity when they negotiated SALT I (Strategic Arms Limitations Treaty) in 1972. It limited the number of land- and submarine-launched missiles and established procedures for modernization. It also limited antiballistic missiles sites (ABM) to two, but they were so ineffective that the United States abandoned its only site in 1975. Underlying SALT I was an acknowledgment of the MAD doctrine.

Compared to the forces of the late 1930s, the enlarged military after World War II demanded a larger officer corps. Draftees filled the privates' ranks, and the NCOs were a mix of combat veterans and some draftees and enlistees. While most of the new officers had extensive combat and wartime experience, many lacked the professional floor that the service academies or ROTC provided. In addition, the huge wartime expansion forced many officers to jump far up in rank and miss service schools that were the backbone of the interwar military establishment.

It was imperative that the military retain high-quality officers and NCOs for careers, especially in a world of sophisticated technology. To do so, the government had to make military service more appealing. It improved pay and the quality of life for service personnel and their families. Before World War II, NCOs were discouraged from marrying or having families. In the 1950s, the military provided better housing, superior benefits, improved schooling for children, and other perks. A family-friendly military offered them a more appealing career.

The most dramatic transformation occurred with the Strategic Air Command (SAC). Founded in 1946, SAC controlled land-based missiles and long-range bombers, both of which carried nuclear weapons. When Lt. Gen. Curtis LeMay took command of SAC, everything changed. From his headquarters in Nebraska, LeMay imposed a culture of checklists, regimentation, and uniformity that was known as SAC culture. The object was to prevent accidents and enhance success by ensuring that everyone followed proper procedures at all times. This overarching structure spilled over into the personal lives of officers and enlisted men on base, and as SAC grew to dominate the Air Force under the New Look, its culture affected most air force personnel and families. While the United States had a few close calls, it never had a major military nuclear accident, and much of that credit belongs to LeMay and his SAC culture.

Since the Treaty of Versailles, Vietnamese nationalist Nguyen Tat Thanh (Ho Chi Minh) and a group of countrymen had sought help from American presidents for an independent Vietnam. During World War II, they fought Japanese occupation and even befriended some U.S. intelligence officials. Despite the Atlantic Charter, the United States helped restore France's prewar status. Vietnam was a pawn in the struggle to rejuvenate France as a world power to counterbalance Soviet strength.

Nonetheless, Ho and his supporters created the Democratic Republic of Vietnam (DRV) in the north and tried to oust the French, while southern Vietnam, more diverse economically, had stronger ties to France and did not join the fight. The United States offered monetary support to buttress France and check communist expansion; Mao's China funneled resources to Ho, making Vietnam both a postcolonial and a Cold War struggle. Momentum in the war ebbed and flowed until early 1954, when North Vietnam captured 20,000 French troops at Dien Bien Phu. By the terms of the Geneva Accords, the DRV controlled the area north of the 17th Parallel, and a pro-Western government led the area south of it. They were to hold elections within two years to decide the country's fate, but neither side pressed for a vote, both fearing the consequences. While the United States became the new patron of South Vietnam, North Vietnamese insurgents infiltrated southward to join South Vietnamese communists.

Like other experts, Eisenhower embraced the Domino Theory: if South Vietnam fell to communism, so would the rest of Indochina, Australia, and New Zealand. Over the next seven years, the United States poured $1 billion in military and economic aid to buttress Ngo Dinh Diem, a corrupt, authoritarian, yet anti-communist leader. U.S. support, however, did not discourage North Vietnam from stepping up its infiltration of the South. Many North Vietnamese came through neighboring Laos and Cambodia (a pathway known as the Ho Chi Minh Trail) and coordinated with local insurgents, the Viet Cong (VC).

When Kennedy assumed the presidency in 1961, he appointed Robert S. McNamara, the president of Ford Motor Company, as secretary of defense. McNamara instituted important budgetary changes that quantified information and permitted cost-effectiveness comparisons of various weapons systems. Together, they stepped up U.S. military presence and support for South Vietnam. Kennedy rejected the New Look and massive retaliation as too restrictive and sought a military capability called "flexible response," meeting communist expansion on all levels—nuclear, conventional, and low intensity. By late 1962, Kennedy had nearly tripled U.S. military strength in Vietnam and established a headquarters, Military Assistance Command Vietnam (MACV).

Although the Army of the Republic of Vietnam (ARVN) exhibited some signs of improvement, Diem's corrupt and ineffective policies negated the success. Diem ordered the Strategic Hamlet Program, moving peasants off traditional homelands and into villages, protected by troops and barbed wire. Yet he did not reform land holdings, and as protests against the government increased, he grew more authoritarian. Diem unnecessarily antagonized Buddhists, who constituted 70 percent of the population, and when others joined their protests, he cracked down once again. As Diem's regime gained new enemies, the insurgency strengthened. The Kennedy administration lost patience with Diem, and it approved a coup attempt. When Diem and his brother were assassinated, however, Kennedy was truly shocked. Three weeks later, he too was assassinated. The coup in South Vietnam spawned countercoups and created more instability.

Kennedy's successor, Lyndon B. Johnson, inherited an impending crisis. Unfortunately, he did not have the knowledge, temperament, military structure, or agenda to deal with it. Johnson mistrusted military leadership, particularly the JCS, and possessed a grossly inflated view of his own capacity as commander in chief. Worse, the divided command authority among the services in Vietnam funneled decision-making back to the White House. Johnson enhanced U.S. military strength to keep South Vietnam from collapsing, yet he feared that the mobilization of National Guardsmen or reservists would damage support and funding for his policies at home: an expansive domestic agenda called the Great Society, including an aggressive civil rights plan and a War on Poverty.

In January 1964, Johnson installed Gen. William Westmoreland as MACV commander. Westmoreland confronted a resilient enemy who skillfully exploited the corrupt and unstable government in South Vietnam. He sought a strategy that would provide security for the people, fortify an unsteady government, and defeat the enemy. He would combine search-and-destroy missions with pacification. To work, though, Westmoreland would need a massive increase in manpower and materiel.

Fortunately for Johnson, a North Vietnamese attack opened the door to military expansion. In August 1964, three North Vietnamese patrol boats attacked a U.S. intelligence-gathering destroyer in neutral waters. Two days later the United States claimed a second attack, which subsequent investigation proved false. Nonetheless, Congress passed the Tonkin Gulf Resolution almost unanimously, granting Johnson a blank check to prevent further aggression.

Johnson remained cautious through his election in 1964, but in February 1965, after the VC attacked a U.S. base at Pleiku, he expanded the scope of the war. He began bombing North Vietnam and escalated troop strength to implement Westmoreland's strategy. By the end of 1965, U.S. forces in Vietnam reached 184,000, and they continued to climb, peaking in early 1969 at 543,400.

As Johnson ratcheted up the war effort, however, the United States confronted the limits of its power. A logical strategy was to

9. Obscured by the elephant grass, U.S. paratroopers turn toward sounds of sniper fire. Behind them, helicopters, a prominent feature of the Vietnam War, depart the area north of Saigon.

attack North Vietnam, but in March 1965, the PRC made clear that it would intervene if the United States invaded North Vietnam. Instead, B-52 bombers dumped heavy payloads on North Vietnam, but contrary to strategic bombing doctrine, they achieved little. Although bombers knocked out power plants and fuel depots, North Vietnam compensated with human power to move goods across the Chinese border or through the jungles of Laos and Cambodia. Against American airmen, the USSR and the PRC installed and manned anti-aircraft guns. Because Johnson limited the targets for fear of drawing the Soviet Union or the PRC into the conflict, pilots needed direct authorization from Washington to strike them.

To achieve security, Westmoreland ordered search-and-destroy missions. More U.S. troops led and fought, and fatalities increased. In 1966, U.S. soldiers who were killed in action rose tenfold; in 1967 that number nearly tripled, and it doubled again in 1968. They relied on greater firepower and technology, which resulted in widespread destruction and deaths of the very civilians the United States was supposed to secure. The Viet Cong and North Vietnam Army (NVA) adapted to counteract U.S. technology. In time they learned that bad weather, disciplined fire, and strong defensive positions enabled them to check the mobility of the helicopter. By clinging to the U.S. and ARVN forces, they largely neutralized the advantages of bombardment and artillery fire, and humans kept fighters supplied with little interruption from U.S. bombers.

Although Westmoreland planned a two-pronged approach, many career officers viewed pacification as duty with no rewards. With DOD fixated on quantifiable assessments, and an enemy that pressured and then eased resistance, MACV adopted no sound means of evaluating pacification efforts. Whether qualified or not, every officer sought combat commands to "check the box" and gain promotions. With McNamara's focus on data, body counts became the critical method of determining success. Commanders and their staffs conjured or inflated enemy killed to position themselves for promotions. Junior officers and enlisted men observed with disgust the spurious body counts, which damaged their faith in many ranking officers, undermined morale, and undercut support for the war.

Back home, the war grew steadily unpopular. Young people in the 1960s embraced a counterculture movement and opposed conformist behavior and opinions. They demanded civil rights for women, Blacks, and Latins, questioned authority, and challenged conventional thought, including the threat of communism. To them, the idea that Vietnam could endanger the American way of life was ridiculous, yet the United States killed hundreds of thousands of Vietnamese and sent young Americans to fight and die in a cause that was not worthwhile. Despite their deferments from the draft, college students took the lead. In 1965, teach-ins on the Vietnam War spread to college campuses across the country, and some 15,000 protesters marched on Washington. The following February, the Senate held hearings on the war where numerous generals and George Kennan called for a withdrawal. Fourteen months later, 100,000 rallied in protest in New York, and on college campuses demonstrations turned violent when authorities tried to break up sit-ins and picket lines. Shaken by the lack of progress and rising opposition, some war advisers stepped down and privately conceded that Vietnam was unwinnable in the current climate.

The military, too, reflected those tensions. Many Black soldiers resented the notion of risking their lives for foreigners when their own society and government refused them equal rights and opportunities. While they did not serve in combat or lose their lives in battle disproportionately, that was their perception, and it influenced race relations. Poorer Whites were compelled to serve while their wealthier countrymen received deferments for college or fake health ailments, generating class hostility. Once it became clear that the United States was not going to win in Vietnam, discipline among many soldiers broke down, and drug use soared, mimicking the behavior of peers back home. The individual rotation system worsened problems, as unit cohesion eroded and officers and enlisted personnel counted the days until they returned home.

By late 1967, Westmoreland and other administration officials believed a positive end was in sight. Less than two months later, the NVA and VC launched a massive surprise offensive that coincided with the Vietnamese New Year, Tet. Well-coordinated attacks struck 100 cities and towns and penetrated the U.S. embassy grounds. Over the next month, U.S. and ARVN forces repulsed them, inflicting immense casualties, but the damage was done. The heavy loss of life and the surprising enemy strength convinced many Americans that the Johnson administration and the military had been lying about wartime progress. By the end of March, opposition was so strong that Johnson announced he would not run for re-election. Both presidential nominees, Republican Richard Nixon and Democrat Hubert Humphrey, promised an end to the Vietnam War.

As president, Nixon tried to play both sides. His administration embraced a policy called Vietnamization—gradually withdrawing under public pressure and turning the war over to the South Vietnamese—which none of his senior officials believed would work. Nixon supported pacification and security yet still relied on firepower and some large operations. He also covertly expanded the war into Laos and Cambodia against congressional prohibition. The North Vietnamese rebuilt their strength. Then, in March 1972, they launched the Easter Offensive, hoping to influence the war and the upcoming the presidential election. Once again, U.S. and South Vietnamese forces repelled the attacks.

Unlike his predecessors, Nixon did not view communism as monolithic. He knew North Vietnam's patrons had larger concerns, and he leveraged their responses by dangling something the Soviet Union and China wanted. Both Nixon and Soviet general secretary Leonid Brezhnev sought a peaceful coexistence, called détente. With a SALT agreement looming as the greater prize for the Soviets, Nixon mined Haiphong harbor to block supplies from entering North Vietnam. The Soviets barely reacted. For China, Nixon agreed to visit and opened relations, and in return China pressured North Vietnam to negotiate seriously. Although North Vietnam resisted, it ultimately yielded. By early 1973, the United States and the DRV signed the Paris Peace Accords, ending U.S. fighting. Two years later, North Vietnam overran South Vietnam and unified the country. The United States did nothing to help its ally.

The United States suffered 47,000 killed in combat, and more than 58,000 died in the war. Another 153,000 Americans were wounded, and more than 1,600 are still missing. Several million Vietnamese soldiers and civilians perished in the fighting.

The impact of the war in the United States was far greater than the disastrous casualties. The American people lost faith in their government and institutions. In March 1968, American soldiers massacred hundreds of civilians and gang-raped women in a village called My Lai. The Army covered it up until a journalist broke the story in November 1969. Only a single lieutenant was found guilty, and the government released him after serving less than four years. In 1970, the public learned that the United States had launched a secret, illegal invasion of Cambodia. Protests erupted on college campuses, and at Kent State University the Ohio National Guard fired into the crowd, killing four and wounding nine. The following year, the *New York Times* published portions of the multivolume *Pentagon Papers*, an internal Defense Department study that revealed the U.S. government had deliberately lied to the public about the progress of the war. That, along with the Watergate affair and other issues, bred widespread distrust of the government and the military. Presidents and their staffs made wrong decisions and misled the American people, and military leaders offered poor recommendations and failed to object in counsel to misguided policies, planning, and decisions, costing more American lives.

In reaction to the war, the U.S. government implemented important changes that altered American military obligations and its personnel. In 1969, Nixon issued the Nixon Doctrine that declared the United States would provide a nuclear umbrella and economic and military assistance but that nations must assume primary responsibility for their own defense against communist aggression. Four years later, Nixon announced a termination of the draft. The military would only accept volunteers, and with poor public opinion of the military, armed forces attracted recruits with behavioral problems and low levels of education. Congress renounced the precedent of the Tonkin Gulf Resolution by passing the War Powers Resolution, requiring the president to notify Congress of the deployment of military personnel in combat areas and to obtain congressional support or withdraw them in sixty days.

Fortunately, a core of devoted officers and NCOs in all the services stayed the course. They analyzed wartime problems, refocused the mission, and incorporated changes in military schools and the ranks that improved morale and effectiveness. In time, they squeezed out troublemakers and incompetents and trained enlisted personnel vigorously, instilling pride in them. Led by a cluster of thoughtful officers with extensive combat experience, the armed forces focused on war against the Soviet bloc in Europe. They instituted new methods of training, relied on fresh technology for realistic maneuvers, and formulated innovative doctrine for fighting. They revamped the military.

No branch suffered more in Vietnam than the army, and none instituted more profound changes in the ensuing fifteen years. Gen. Creighton Abrams, who succeeded Westmoreland as MACV commander and then chief of staff, brokered an agreement with the secretary of defense for a sixteen-division army with no new infusion of personnel. To fill it, Abrams shifted combat support responsibilities to the reserves and National Guard. For the government to deploy a division in combat, it would have to mobilize reserves and guardsmen, thereby triggering public debate over involvement. After his death in 1974, Abrams's closest subordinates carried on the revival. They established laser training devices to increase realism, built the National Training Center in California for large-scale maneuvers and testing, and formulated a new doctrine called AirLand Battle, a joint approach to conventional warfighting that emphasized initiative, deep strikes, agility, and firepower.

The military revival was incomplete until Ronald Reagan's presidency. The combination of the Vietnam War, Johnson's Great

Society, and soaring oil prices led to inflation that peaked at 14 percent in 1980. President Jimmy Carter tried to check inflation by reducing the deficit, including freezing the defense budget. Although he increased defense spending the last two years, those changes were lost amid the Soviet invasion of Afghanistan and the Iran hostage crisis, when the United States stood powerless as Iranians seized and held 52 U.S. government personnel and citizens for 444 days. Reagan campaigned on a platform for a revived economy and a stronger military and he won a landslide victory in 1980.

Once in office, Reagan cut taxes, especially for the wealthy, reduced the size of the government, but dramatically increased the defense budget 35 percent. Although the massive infusion of defense dollars resulted in waste, military personnel suddenly received pay raises, better weapons and equipment, stockpiles of ammunition, and more training time. Morale leaped as the administration lavished resources, attention, and praise on the troops. Better-educated civilians, frustrated by the stagnant economy, joined in droves, and the quality of enlisted personnel improved dramatically, a necessity with increasingly sophisticated technology.

The role of women in the military expanded as well. Highly qualified females joined the armed forces, shattering the traditional ceilings by assuming duties that were once the exclusive domain of males. As the vastness of the battlefield expanded, they found themselves more and more under fire, and their outstanding performance opened new doors. In 2013, the DOD ordered that all jobs be opened to qualified women. By 2017, women were training in infantry units, one of the last bastions of military masculinity.

As the U.S. military improved and the Soviets got bogged down in Afghanistan in the 1980s, the new Soviet general secretary, Mikhail Gorbachev, worried that the technology gap between the

United States and the Soviet Union was growing exponentially. The only way the Soviets could keep up, he believed, was by adopting *glasnost*, greater openness in society, to encourage and promote technological and scientific improvements. Gorbachev and Reagan negotiated the Strategic Arms Reduction Treaty (START), limiting strategic nuclear delivery systems to 1,600 and warheads to 6,000, but Reagan's proposed Strategic Defense Initiative (SDI, or Star Wars), the development of weapons to shoot down ICBMs from platforms in space, incited Gorbachev's greatest fear. SDI would neutralize Soviet ICBMs and make that nation defenseless against U.S. attacks. Gorbachev proposed that both nations eliminate all nuclear weapons. Reagan declined.

Shortages and turmoil crumbled the undergirding of Soviet domestic structure as the transition from a controlled to a market economy took time. In Eastern Europe, the loosening resulted in the rapid collapse of communist regimes, followed by waves of democratic movements. In November 1989, the Berlin Wall fell, and the other Soviet-dominated states toppled like dominoes. By late 1991, the remnants of the Soviet Union collapsed, bringing an end to the Cold War.

Despite the infusion of funds, the U.S. military did not turn itself around overnight. In October 1983, a suicide bomber blew up a Marine barracks in Beirut, Lebanon, killing 241 Americans who were part of a UN peacekeeping mission. Sensible rules of engagement and basic precautions would most likely have spared many of those lives. Two days later, after a revolutionary group had overthrown the existing government in Grenada, the United States launched a joint invasion to restore the government and liberate American students there. Resistance was light, and the United States seized the island, but the poor coordination among the services might have proved disastrous against a stronger enemy.

The following year, the Reagan administration suggested the conditions and manner in which it would deploy troops. Named after Secretary of Defense Caspar Weinberger, the Weinberger Doctrine argued that vital interests should be at stake, political and military objectives should be clearly defined, military forces should be sized to achieve the objectives, there should be reasonable public support for military actions, and U.S. forces should be committed only as a last resort. The goal was to avoid another Vietnam.

In 1986, the United States finally addressed an issue that had plagued the military since World War II: unified command in joint operations. Joint warfighting required joint commands under a single commander. To deal with the problem, Congress passed the Goldwater-Nichols Act, the most sweeping change in the command structure since the National Security Act of 1947. The law placed clear responsibilities and authority on unified and specified commands for planning, joint resources, and execution and it enhanced the powers of the chairman of the JCS at the expense of service chiefs, whose duties were largely limited to training and equipping troops in their service.

In its initial trial, the invasion of Panama to seize the dictator and drug trafficker Manuel Noriega, Goldwater-Nichols worked well, but the real test was the First Gulf War. Saddam Hussein, the ruler of Iraq, invaded Kuwait in August 1990 without provocation to increase Iraq's oil reserves, wealth, and power. With the fall of Kuwait, Iraq posed a threat to Saudi Arabia. The ensuing instability in the Middle East and the threat to oil supplies in the West prompted President George H. W. Bush to assume a leadership role. He lobbied the UN to pass Resolution 678, condemning the invasion of Kuwait and demanding Iraqi withdrawal by mid-January 1991, and he built a coalition force with thirty-two nations contributing personnel.

Even though Iraq had 500,000 defenders and modern Soviet-made equipment, the coalition built up a force of 800,000. Of those, 500,000 were American personnel with the most up-to-date equipment. Bush mobilized Reserve and National Guard units, ensuring broad participation and expanded public interest. It became a 24-hour-a-day "television war."

Responsibility rested with Central Command (CENTCOM) head Gen. Norman Schwarzkopf, a talented but irascible officer with a "shoot-the-messenger" temperament. The strain that Schwarzkopf and his top service subordinates felt was worsened when the Air Force and Marine Corps high command pressured them for expanded roles. Neither service fully embraced Goldwater-Nichols, but CENTCOM won the day with support from Gen. Colin Powell, chairman of the JCS, and the Bush administration.

On January 15, 1991, coalition forces began forty-one days of airstrikes, targeting Iraqi air defense and command and control, and then shifting to energy, supply, and defensive positions. On February 24, the ground campaign began. Feigning an amphibious landing, the Marines drove the enemy into Kuwait City. On the opposite flank, the coalition forces launched a wide left hook through the desert. With extraordinary logistical support, the attack roared across the Iraqi terrain and crashed down on the enemy's flank. Like the air war, superior weapons, vehicles, and training paid huge dividends. Coalition forces crushed the Iraqis, suffering 240 battlefield fatalities and killing 10,000 combatants and 2,000 civilians. The ground war ended in 100 hours, with the Iraqis routed from Kuwait.

Throughout the crisis, the Bush administration walked a tightrope, preserving a diverse coalition that included much of the Arab world. When Iraq began firing SCUD missiles into Israel, the United States' closest partner in the region, to provoke retaliation and destroy Arab support for the war, Bush secured Israeli restraint. He also halted before launching a full-scale invasion of

Iraq. Footage of U.S. forces destroying convoys of vehicles and personnel fleeing to Iraq disturbed some Arab allies, while others feared the destruction of Iraq would leave Iran as the dominant power in the region. With no real choice, Iraq accepted the terms of the ceasefire, which included reparations; destruction of its biological, chemical, and nuclear weapons programs; and a no-fly zone. The agreement limited trade with Iraq until it met all terms. Unfortunately, the terms permitted armed helicopter flights in Iraq, which Saddam used to suppress Kurdish uprisings.

To a great extent, the Gulf War vanquished the ghosts of Vietnam. Iraq engaged the United States and its allies in exactly the kind of conflict that the post-Vietnam military trained and upgraded to fight: a conventional war. The American public cheered its military, and not since World War II had the armed forces felt such a sense of pride in its accomplishments, nor had the public felt so proud of its armed forces. Yet what also emerged from the triumph was a fairly widespread conviction among officers, politicians, and intellectuals that new technology had so transformed warfare—Revolution in Military Affairs—that past practices were valueless. It proved to be a severely misguided notion.

To the dismay of many experts, Bush's successor as president, Bill Clinton, knew little about the military before taking office. He drew down the armed forces to 1.4 million and earned the ire of many military personnel and veterans by trying to end the ban on homosexuals in uniform. After much wrangling, Clinton and Congress created "Don't Ask, Don't Tell," a strange compromise that allowed gays to serve. No one was allowed to ask, and the person did not have to tell. It lasted until 2011, when a survey indicated most military personnel cared little about homosexuality in the services and Congress lifted the ban.

Yet Clinton also oversaw a huge budgetary increase to $318 billion and avoided major conventional operations. He continued Bush's limited commitment with the UN to Somalia, which ended disastrously at Mogadishu, and ordered the United States to participate in a frustrating UN peacekeeping mission in Haiti. Later, however, the United States joined NATO forces to restore order in Bosnia. It retrained the Bosnian army and aided it with airstrikes against Serbian forces to end Serbian ethnic cleansing operations in the former Yugoslavia and attacks against UN forces. Unfortunately, it fortified the conviction among selected officers, politicians, and intellectuals that precision-guided weapons and other technologies—the Revolution in Military Affairs—made extensive ground forces unnecessary.

On September 11, 2001, al-Qaeda terrorists struck the United States. Upset over American forces stationed in the Middle East after the First Gulf War, jihadists hijacked planes and crashed them into the World Trade Center, the Pentagon, and the Pennsylvania countryside, killing nearly 3,000 people. U.S. intelligence tracked the plan to al-Qaeda and its head, a Saudi named Osama bin Laden, who found sanctuary in Afghanistan, where Muslim extremists known as the Taliban held power. President George W. Bush promptly declared a global war on terror and demanded the Taliban surrender bin Laden. When it refused, he took steps to invade Afghanistan and crush al-Qaeda.

Not since the Japanese attack on Pearl Harbor had passions so seized the American public. Citizens demanded action, and young adults thronged to recruiting centers to join the armed forces. Congress gave Bush complete authority to hunt down the 9/11 plotters, and NATO declared 9/11 an attack that required military assistance from all member nations. Internally, the United States recognized 9/11 as a failure to share information among various intelligence agencies. In response, Congress created the Department of Homeland Security to oversee public security and coordinate among various agencies, and it dramatically expanded the national security system.

In October 2001, the United States invaded Afghanistan. Supported by anti-Taliban Afghans, the United States toppled the Taliban government within five months. Yet the achievement was not as simple or complete as U.S. officials believed. The speed of the victory and the skillful airstrikes with precision-guided bombs and drones gave civilian and some military leaders a false sense of easy victories. Bin Laden and 1,000 followers retreated to the Pakistani border area called Tora Bora, where they found refuge amid caves and defensive positions. Drones and air strikes could not destroy them, and logistics, difficult terrain, and weather discouraged U.S. commander Gen. Tommy Franks from injecting more ground troops into Tora Bora. Ultimately, bin Laden and 800 al-Qaeda supporters escaped to Pakistan, where that government made halfhearted efforts to uproot them.

The Bush administration did not want to get bogged down in nation building, and it imposed strict limitations on troop strength. It called on allies to create a stable, democratic government, while U.S. military personnel concentrated on building a strong Afghan army and rooting out al-Qaeda elements. The United States would rely on technological superiority, a concept that demonstrated its weakness once again in March 2002 at Shah-i-Kot, near the Pakistan border. Some 500 to 1,000 well-supplied al-Qaeda and foreign jihadists drove back anti-Taliban militia, and American ground spotters could not communicate to air force pilots by radio.

In the aftermath of Shah-i-Kot, the Bush administration began withdrawing troops, especially Special Forces, for use in Iraq, but the fighting was far from over. For many Afghans, poverty and destruction worsened, breeding greater unrest, and warlords, who wielded local power, blocked reform unless it benefited them. Money from the opium trade corrupted politicians and soured the people's hopes of any positive changes. Most Taliban leaders escaped, and many of its fighters blended into communities; al-Qaeda survived in Pakistan or along its Afghanistan border.

With limited resources, coalition power focused on urban areas and conceded the countryside, as opposition elements increased their strength and attacked and dominated selected areas. Stability in Afghanistan deteriorated steadily. Coalition operations shifted from counterterrorism to counterinsurgency, yet the limited number of forces, the restrictive rules of engagement that the UN imposed upon them, and the unwillingness of Pakistan to challenge insurgents in their country prevented coalition forces from eliminating them.

Meanwhile, the United States shifted its focus to Iraq. A large group of intellectuals, politicians, and lobbyists known as neocons (neoconservatives) joined with Vice President Richard Cheney, Secretary of Defense Donald Rumsfeld, and Deputy Secretary Paul Wolfowitz in a plan to complete unfinished business from the First Gulf War, destroying Saddam Hussein and creating a model democracy for the Arab world in Iraq. They justified the campaign by arguing that Iraq had failed to live up to the terms of the ceasefire agreement, Saddam was cultivating ties with al-Qaeda (a claim later proved false), and Iraq was aggressively seeking weapons of mass destruction that would destabilize a troubled region (American troops eventually discovered dated chemical weapons).

Rumsfeld and Wolfowitz scrapped military plans for a major troop buildup and instead planned an invasion with just 160,000 troops (mostly U.S. forces), and precision bombing and other air strikes. Rumsfeld and Wolfowitz believed the coalition would oust Saddam by "shock and awe," paving the way for a democracy at a very low cost in American lives, treasure, and time. They expected a reception as liberators, not invaders. Unfortunately, neither man took to heart Thucydides's warning that people think they can control war but war controls them. They believed wholeheartedly in their own plans and failed to consider alternatives and contingencies. They were convinced that Iraqi oil revenues, at the time around $15–20 billion annually, would pay for the war. And they devoted little thought to the postwar situation. When Army Chief of Staff Gen. Eric Shinseki told a congressional committee that the coalition would need several hundred thousand troops for occupation duty, Wolfowitz called the projection "wildly off the mark." They then shunned Shinseki, earning widespread hostility among the armed forces and building a wall between civilian and military leadership.

Rumsfeld and Wolfowitz trapped themselves by insisting the war would be comparatively inexpensive. The military did not have the 300,000 men and women necessary for the occupation, and to mobilize more Reservists and National Guard units would have raised the tab and quickly provoked public dissatisfaction for a war that was not vital to U.S. interests. "These are educated men, they are smart men," a general said of Rumsfeld and Wolfowitz. "But they are not wise men."

On March 20, 2003, coalition forces struck swiftly. Organized resistance largely dissolved, but Saddam's militia and some Iraqi forces began harassing allied troops. In early April, U.S. forces penetrated Baghdad. Five months later, they took Saddam prisoner. What Rumsfeld, Wolfowitz, and General Franks failed to anticipate, however, was a widespread guerrilla war. Saddam's strong-arm tactics installed the minority Sunni Muslims in power, kept the majority Shi'a Muslims subdued, and quieted the rebellious Kurds. Once he was removed, civil violence erupted. With Iranian support, Shi'a militias formed and fought Sunnis and occupation forces. When Paul Bremer, the top American civilian official in Iraq, disbanded the Iraqi army and fired all members of Saddam's Baath Party, many of them joined the fight against the occupiers and Shia militias. In the First Gulf War, Islamic nations either supported the allied cause publicly or gave a silent nod and remained neutral. In the second war, foreigners had invaded Iraq without overt provocation, and Muslims were outraged. Islamic jihadists poured into Iraq, attempting to oust the Americans and seize power and wealth for their jihadist cause.

The Bush administration did not expect such a hostile reception. The destructive nature of American firepower, deprivations of food and electricity, and widespread danger and violence alienated even those who loathed Saddam and his regime. The United States lacked sufficient occupation forces to protect the people and guard the weapons and ammunition dumps, which Iraqis and jihadists plundered. Brutality and violence against Iraqis— especially torture and humiliation of prisoners by U.S. Army reservists at Abu Ghraib—generated more enemies, many of whom targeted American convoys and troops. With no anticipation of a guerrilla war, losses were heavy. Most U.S. troops lacked body armor for protection, and vehicles needed reinforced steel plating to shield troops from improvised explosive devices (IEDs). Once again, inexpensive alternatives like IEDs neutralized armored vehicles. Officers and enlisted personnel, trained in conventional warfare, struggled initially to adapt. American forces did adjust, and most understood the consequences of mistreating locals, but one act of poor judgment overrode weeks of goodwill. What seemed like a quick victory suddenly appeared to be a military quagmire, and the preventive war squandered worldwide sympathy toward the United States over 9/11.

In 2006, however, signs of improvement occurred. Sunnis were irritated with the extent of violence that foreign insurgents committed against fellow Iraqis and wanted them gone. They began working with the Americans to oust al-Qaeda from Iraq. Iran discovered that it could work with the Iraqi leadership and pressured Shi'a militias to quit killing Sunnis. Religious groups segregated in urban areas, and that reduced clashes as well.

The United States followed those changes with two major developments. In December 2006, a new counterinsurgency manual helped guide junior officers and NCOs in their operations and approaches to problem solving. The next year, Bush authorized a surge of troops into Iraq. Led by Gen. David Petraeus, this increase in "boots on the ground," raising

U.S. strength to nearly 158,000, came at just the right time to subdue most of the remaining insurgents and to restore protection and some order.

In 2009, Barack Obama, the new president, had pledged to end the Iraq War. Obama continued the drawdown that Bush initiated, shifting many more troops back to Afghanistan. Attempts to negotiate a long-term deal with Iraq failed, and the United States evacuated its troops by 2011, leaving a token force that helped train Iraqis. Trouble with the Islamic State of Iraq and Syria (ISIS) convinced Obama to send 500 more troops into Iraq in 2016, and the United States stepped up bombing and drone attacks in Syria to aid American-supported ground troops, driving ISIS from much of the territory it occupied. In 2019, President Donald Trump announced a withdrawal, creating a power vacuum that Syria, Russia's surrogate, filled and exposing the Kurds, who successfully fought ISIS, to Turkish devastation.

Despite the predictions of Rumsfeld and Wolfowitz, the cost of war in Iraq was staggering. Nearly 5,000 U.S. troops were killed in action, and tens of thousands more suffered physical or psychological wounds. Estimates of Iraqis killed vary from 109,000 to more than 1 million. The Congressional Research Service maintains that the war in Iraq cost $815 billion, although other experts estimate the cost for the United States at $1.7 trillion. It also damaged the United States' reputation in international circles. Rather than serve as a springboard to democracy in the Middle East, the war inspired religious extremist groups that have bred death, destruction, and chaos throughout the region.

After witnessing significant improvement in Iraq due in part to a troop increase, Bush officials attempted a surge in Afghanistan. While officers and troops focused on community building whenever possible, the inevitable rise in violence and destruction infuriated the Afghan government. President Hamid Karzai demanded an immediate halt to home searches, unnecessary detentions, and airstrikes amid civilian targets, which was where the insurgents lived. Logistics, too, became more problematic. As the number of troops increased, the Pakistani government periodically halted shipments in protest of bombing and drone strikes without its approval. The United States withheld information because Pakistani leaks alerted insurgents.

Obama had pledged to complete the task of crushing al-Qaeda in Afghanistan. Unfortunately, an increase in insurgent attacks convinced U.S. allies to remove their personnel. Obama augmented the existing forces with 30,000 troops, but he also set a withdrawal date for all U.S. combat forces by 2014. He wanted no more open-ended military commitments.

Obama turned to a Petraeus acolyte, Gen. Stanley McChrystal, to head the war in Afghanistan. A counterinsurgency expert, McChrystal concentrated troops on improving the lives of the Afghan people by providing medical care, schools, and economic opportunities. He reminded U.S. forces to conduct themselves properly at all times and not to tolerate corrupt governments. He also placed Special Forces in villages to help train local police and coordinate protection with district and provincial forces.

But for all his good work, McChrystal foolishly allowed a writer for *Rolling Stone* to follow him for several days, and McChrystal's staff criticized and disrespected political leaders in front of the writer and the general. It was McChrystal's second major gaffe— he leaked information to the media—and in the interest of civilian control of the military, McChrystal resigned. In May 2011, the U.S. government finally brought to a close the manhunt for bin Laden. A SEAL (Sea, Air, and Land) team raided bin Laden's compound in Pakistan and shot and killed him. It also discovered a trove of priceless intelligence that aided the war against al-Qaeda.

10. Command Sgt. Maj. Jack Stanford and Col. Gail Yoshitani escorted visitors reporting on how U.S. Special Forces teams were doing in terms of village stability operations and training Afghan local police. Col. Yoshitani wears a hijab out of respect for the local culture, which was critical in gaining the support of locals.

Violence in Afghanistan continued, as did tension between the United States and the Afghan governments. These problems accelerated the arrangement to turn over more responsibilities to the Afghanis. Still, the two parties were able to negotiate a deal to keep 15,000 coalition forces in Afghanistan, and in June 2016 Obama authorized U.S. troops to enter combat with Afghan forces. As of 2016, the United States had lost more than 2,200 dead, over 1,800 of those in combat, and more than 20,000 suffered wounds. The war in Afghanistan alone cost approximately $700 billion and is compounding.

In 2017, with the election of Donald Trump as president, attention has shifted once again. Classified documents released by WikiLeaks and cyberattacks emanating from Russia attempted to

Conclusion: The armed forces and perennial problems

For 400 years, the American military has struggled with balancing a standing army with citizen soldier, enhancing military professionalism, the development and utilization of technology, and understanding the limits of its power. Even today, those issues play a major role in the armed forces and the government's policies toward them.

The wars in Afghanistan and Iraq merely highlight some serious problems with the all-volunteer force. Most of those who serve in the military have family ties to the armed forces or are from poorer backgrounds. Most politicians who are sending Americans into danger have no family in uniform. Politicians need to apply greater circumspection before risking American lives and remember that these are someone's children, spouses, parents, or siblings.

Most Americans contributed absolutely nothing to the wars in Afghanistan and Iraq. They had no family members deploy, paid no extra taxes to fund the wars, and over time lost interest. Politicians realized that if the wars affected few families, then resistance to them would be minimal. The problem is that in war a comparative few usually bear the greatest sacrifice, but everyone must shoulder some burden. Because leaders assumed the wars would be quick, inexpensive, and limited, they did not plan properly for returning veterans. Advanced medical technology enables the military to save more lives, but those veterans often need extensive medical attention. Veterans who did suffer wounds and those who did not but witnessed the horrors of war return home to very few people with whom they can share experiences, and they require skilled counseling to adjust to civilian life. Others emerge from military service with no skills and limited job prospects, a hard pill to swallow after fighting for their country. Experts estimate that long-term care for veterans of Iraq and Afghanistan will cost $4 to $6 trillion, which future generations will have to pay.

Politicians and many officers assumed that new technology had changed warfare monumentally and that they were confronting a brave new world. They convinced themselves that this new technology enabled them to control and shape war. To their peril, they ignored the lessons of Thucydides and others, particularly about the human elements of warfare. Military professionals have an obligation to enhance their knowledge through various mediums. Like other professions, the military needs to cut back on paperwork and inconsequential duties and devote greater time for professional development. In the end, a more professional officer corps will save lives and complete assignments more successfully.

With advantages from technology come problems as well. Computer viruses and other cyber attacks can cripple armed forces at modest expenses to the aggressor. The advent of social media exposed indiscreet acts and comments globally, causing enormous problems and undoing the trust built over time. Inappropriate statements about the commander in chief and other political leaders undermine civilian control of the military and damage the reputation of the armed forces in the eyes of the people whom they are serving. Military personnel are under continual scrutiny and must always be wary of careless talk or imprudent behavior.

Though technology is unquestionably advantageous, enemies discover low-cost ways of neutralizing it. With so much faith placed in technology, leaders assumed an outcome and neglected to plan for contingencies. In the end they had to rely on the tried-and-true "boots on the ground," a much costlier and lengthier approach to warfare.

The United States spends more on defense than the next eight largest nations combined. No doubt, sophisticated technology is vital for national security, and it is very expensive. It is also critical for technological and scientific breakthroughs in the civilian world. At the same time, the United States has competing domestic interests that the government must eventually address, among them expansion and improvement of veterans' care. Whether the United States will or should sustain that level of defense spending will be at the heart of that problem. In 1912, Secretary of War Henry Stimson wrote that the problem with our army was that politicians lacked an effective policy toward it. More than a century later the same could be argued with the armed forces as a whole. In 2003, few people would have predicted that Afghanistan and Iraq would become America's longest wars and would once again confront the limits of power. The United States possesses the finest military force in the world, but sometimes the task is greater than it can fulfill; other times the costs are so great that the results are not worth the price. Although it is important for military leaders to possess a "can-do" attitude, they must also communicate frankly and confidentially to political leaders what duties they can and cannot complete and what the human fallout likely will be. Politicians and the public, moreover, need guidance on what missions the armed forces can and cannot reasonably accomplish. Even though they will confront a clear line in civil-military relations, military professionals need to take the lead in that education process. No one should know that better than they do.

References

Chapter 1

Isaack de Rasières, "New Netherland in 1627," New-York Historical
Society, *Collections*, Series 2, Vol. II (New York: Published for the
Society, 1849), 352.

Washington to Colonel William Woodford, 10 Nov. 1775, in *Writings
of George Washington*, ed. Jared Sparks (Boston: Russell, Odiorne,
and Metcalf and Hilliard, Gray and Company, 1834), 3:151–54.

George Washington, "Sentiments on a Peace Establishment," 1 May
1783. George Washington Papers, Library of Congress.

Washington to John Hancock, 20 Dec. 1776, in *The Papers of George
Washington*, ed. Philander D. Chase, Revolutionary War Series
(Charlottesville: University Press of Virginia, 1997), 7:381–89.

Donald Hickey, *The War of 1812: A Forgotten War* (Urbana: University
of Illinois Press, 2012), 70.

Chapter 2

"Enlisted Men," *Army and Navy Chronicle* 8, no. 24 (June 13,
1839): 382.

Edward M. Coffman, *The Old Army: A Portrait of the American Army
in Peacetime, 1784–1898* (New York: Oxford University Press,
1986), 101.

Milo Milton Quaife, ed., *The Diary of James K. Polk during His
Presidency, 1845–1849*, 3 (Chicago: A. C. McClurg & Co.,
1910), 266.

"A Declaration of the Immediate Causes Which Induce and Justify the Secession of the State of Mississippi from the Federal Union." avalon.law.yale.edu/19th_century/csa_missec.asp.

Joseph T. Glatthaar, *Forged in Battle: The Civil War Alliance of Black Soldiers and White Officers* (New York: Free Press, 1990), 7.

Joseph T. Glatthaar, *Partners in Command: The Relationships between Leaders in the Civil War* (New York: Free Press, 1994), 64.

David F. Trask, *The War with Spain in 1898* (New York: Macmillan, 1981), 221.

Chapter 3

D. Clayton James and Anne Sharp Wells, *America and the Great War, 1914–1920* (Wheeling, IL: Harlan Davison, 1998), 80.

Edward M. Coffman, *The War to End All Wars: The American Military Experience in World War I* (New York: Oxford University Press, 1968), 109.

Allan R. Millett, *Semper Fidelis: A History of the United States Marine Corps* (New York: Free Press, 1991), 301.

"Siberia Is Cooler Than Usual Where Uncle Sam Is Concerned," *Literary Digest* 62, no. 10 (September 6, 1919): 60.

Alfred F. Hurley, *Billy Mitchell: Crusader for Air Power* (Bloomington: Indiana University Press, 1975), 101.

Chapter 4

Lori Lyn Bogle, *The Pentagon's Battle for the American Mind: The Early Cold War* (College Station: Texas A&M University Press, 2004), 51.

Keith D. McFarland, "The 1949 Revolt of the Admirals," *Parameters: The Journal of the U.S. Army War College* 40, no. 2 (1980): 60.

Testimony of General of the Army Omar N. Bradley, Chairman of the Joint Chiefs of Staff to Committees of Senate Armed Services and Foreign Relations, 15 May 1951, *Case Study: The Korean War* (Carlisle Barracks, PA: U.S. Army War College, 1990), IV:4.

Thomas E. Ricks, *Fiasco: The American Military Adventure in Iraq* (New York: Penguin Books, 2006), 97.

Ricks, *Fiasco*, 99.

Further reading

Anderson, Fred. *Crucible of War: The Seven Years' War and the Fate of Empire in British North America, 1754–1766*. New York: Alfred A. Knopf, 2000.

Anderson, Fred. *Dominion of War: Empire and Liberty in North America, 1500–2000*. New York: Viking, 2005.

Anderson, Fred. *A People's Army: Massachusetts Soldiers and Society in the Seven Years' War*. Chapel Hill: University of North Carolina Press, 1984.

Atkinson, Rick. *An Army at Dawn: The War in North Africa, 1942–1943*. New York: Henry Holt, 2002.

Atkinson, Rick. *The Day of Battle: The War in Sicily and Italy, 1943–1944*. New York: Henry Holt, 2007.

Atkinson, Rick. *The Guns at Last Light: The War in Western Europe, 1944–1945*. New York: Henry Holt, 2013.

Atkinson, Rick. *The Long Gray Line*. Boston: Houghton Mifflin, 1986.

Bacevich, Andrew J. *America's War for the Middle East: A Military History*. New York: Random House, 2016.

Bacevich, Andrew J. *Breach of Trust: How Americans Failed Their Soldiers and Their Country*. New York: Metropolitan Books, 2013.

Bacevich, Andrew J. *The Limits of Power: The End of American Exceptionalism*. New York: Metropolitan Books, 2008.

Birtle, Andrew J. *U.S. Army Counterinsurgency and Contingency Operations Doctrine, 1942–1976*. Washington, DC: U.S. Army Center of Military History, 2006.

Brown, John Sloan. *Kevlar Legions: The Transformation of the U.S. Army, 1989–2005*. Washington, DC: U.S. Army Center of Military History, 2011.

Coffman, Edward M. *The Old Army: A Portrait of the American Army in Peacetime, 1784–1899*. New York: Oxford University Press, 1986.

Coffman, Edward M. *The Regulars: The American Army, 1898–1940*. Cambridge, MA: Belknap Press of Harvard University Press, 2004.

Coffman, Edward M. *The War to End All Wars: The American Experience in World War I*. New York: Oxford University Press, 1968.

Copp, DeWitt S. *A Few Great Captains: The Men and Events That Shaped the Development of U.S. Airpower*. Garden City, NY: Doubleday, 1980.

D'Este, Carlo. *Eisenhower: A Soldier's Life*. New York: Henry Holt, 2002.

Drea, Edward J. *Japan's Imperial Army: Its Rise and Fall, 1853–1945*. Lawrence: University Press of Kansas, 2009.

Duval, Kathleen. *Independence Lost: Lives on the Edge of the American Revolution*. New York: Random House, 2015.

Eisenhower, John S. D. *So Far from God: The U.S. War with Mexico, 1846–1848*. New York: Random House, 1989.

Fairweather, Jack. *The Good War: Why We Couldn't Win the War or the Peace in Afghanistan*. New York: Basic Books, 2014.

Faust, Drew Gilpin. *This Republic of Suffering: Death and the American Civil War*. New York: Alfred A. Knopf, 2008.

Gallagher, Gary W. *The Confederate War*. Cambridge, MA: Harvard University Press, 1997.

Gallagher, Gary W. *The Union War*. Cambridge, MA: Harvard University Press, 2011.

Glatthaar, Joseph T. *Forged in Battle: The Civil War Alliance of Black Soldiers and Their White Officers*. New York: Free Press, 1989.

Glatthaar, Joseph T. *General Lee's Army: From Victory to Collapse*. New York: Free Press, 2008.

Glatthaar, Joseph T. *The March to the Sea and Beyond: Union Troops in the Savannah and Carolinas Campaigns*. New York: New York University Press, 1985.

Gordon, Michael R., and Bernard E. Trainor. *The Generals' War: The Inside Story of the Conflict in the Gulf*. Boston: Little, Brown, 1995.

Grimsley, Mark. *The Hard Hand of War: Union Military Policy toward Southern Civilians, 1861–1865*. Cambridge: Cambridge University Press, 1995.

Grotelueschen, Mark E. *The AEF Way of War: The American Army and Combat in World War I*. New York: Cambridge University Press, 2007.

Gruber, Ira D. *Books and the British Army in the Age of the American Revolution*. Chapel Hill: University of North Carolina Press, 2010.

Hickey, Donald R. *The War of 1812: A Forgotten Conflict*. Urbana: University of Illinois Press, 2012.

Higginbotham, R. Don. *The War of American Independence: Military Attitudes, Policies, and Practice, 1763–1789*. New York: Macmillan, 1971.

Hughes, Thomas Alexander. *Admiral Bill Halsey: A Naval Life*. Cambridge, MA: Harvard University Press, 2016.

Hughes, Thomas Alexander. *Overlord: General Pete Quesada and the Triumph of Tactical Airpower in World War II*. New York: Free Press, 1985.

James, D. Clayton. *The Years of MacArthur*. 3 vols. Boston: Houghton Mifflin, 1970–1985.

Karnow, Stanley. *Vietnam: A History*. New York: Penguin, 1991.

Keene, Jennifer D. *Doughboys, the Great War, and the Remaking of America*. Baltimore: Johns Hopkins University Press, 2001.

Kennedy, David M. *Over Here: The First World War and American Society*. New York: Oxford University Press, 2004.

Kitfield, James. *Prodigal Soldiers: How the Generation of Officers Born of Vietnam Revolutionized the American Style of War*. New York: Simon & Schuster, 1995.

Kohn, Richard H. *Eagle and Sword: The Federalists and the Creation of the Military Establishment in America, 1783–1802*. New York: Free Press, 1975.

Lee, Wayne E. *Barbarians and Brothers: Anglo-American Warfare, 1500–1865*. New York: Oxford University Press, 2011.

Lee, Wayne E. *Waging War: Conflict, Culture, and Innovation in World History*. New York: Oxford University Press, 2016.

Leffler, Melvin P. *A Preponderance of Power: National Security, the Truman Administration, and the Cold War*. Palo Alto, CA: Stanford University Press, 1992.

Linn, Brian. *The Echo of Battle: The Army's Way of War*. Cambridge, MA: Harvard University Press, 2007.

Linn, Brian. *Guardians of Empire: U.S. Army and the Pacific, 1902–1940*. Chapel Hill: University of North Carolina Press, 1997.

Linn, Brian. *The Philippine War, 1899–1902*. Lawrence: University Press of Kansas, 2000.

Mackin, Elton. *Suddenly, We Didn't Want to Die: Memoirs of a World War I Marine*. Novato, CA: Presidio Press, 1996.

McMaster, H. R. *Dereliction of Duty: Lyndon Johnson, Robert McNamara, the Joint Chiefs of Staff, and the Lies That Led to Vietnam*. New York: HarperCollins, 1997.

McPherson, James M. *Battle Cry of Freedom: The Civil War Era*. New York: Oxford University Press, 1986.

McPherson, James M. *For Cause and Comrades: Why Men Fought in the Civil War*. New York: Oxford University Press, 1997.

McPherson, James M. *Tried by War: Abraham Lincoln as Commander in Chief*. New York: Penguin, 2008.

Middlekauff, Robert. *The Glorious Cause: The American Revolution, 1763-1789*. New York: Oxford University Press, 2005.

Millett, Allan R. *The General: Robert L. Bullard and Officership in the United States Army, 1881-1925*. Westport, CT: Greenwood Press, 1975.

Millett, Allan R. *Korean War in World History*. Lexington: University Press of Kentucky, 2004.

Millett, Allan R. *Semper Fidelis: The History of the United States Marine Corps*. Rev. ed. New York: Macmillan, 1991.

Millett, Allan R., Peter Maslowski, and William B. Feis. *For the Common Defense: A Military History of the United States from 1607-2012*. 3rd ed. New York: Free Press, 2012.

Millis, Walter. *Arms and Men: A Study in American Military History*. New York: Putnam, 1956.

Moore, Harold G., and Joseph L. Galloway. *We Were Soldiers Once... and Young: Ia Drang—The Battle That Changed the War in Vietnam*. New York: HarperTorch, 2002.

Moten, Matthew. *Presidents & Their Generals: An American History of Command in War*. Cambridge, MA: Belknap Press of Harvard University Press, 2014.

Moten, Matthew, ed. *Between War and Peace: How America Ends Its Wars*. New York: Free Press, 2011.

Pogue, Forrest. *George C. Marshall*. 4 vols. New York: Viking, 1963-1987.

Polenberg, Richard. *America at War: The Home Front, 1941-1945*. Englewood Cliffs, NJ: Prentice-Hall, 1968.

Ricks, Thomas E. *Fiasco: The American Military Adventure in Iraq*. New York: Penguin, 2007.

Ricks, Thomas E. *The Gamble: General David Petraeus and the American Military Adventure in Iraq, 2006-2008*. New York: Penguin, 2009.

Rogers, Clifford J., and Ty Seidule, senior eds. *The West Point History of Warfare*. New York: Rowan Technology Solutions, 2015.

Sheehan, Neil. *A Bright and Shining Lie: John Paul Vann and America in Vietnam*. New York: Random House, 1988.

Sherry, Michael S. *The Rise of American Airpower: The Creation of Armageddon*. New Haven: Yale University Press, 1987.

Shy, John W. *A People Numerous and Armed: Reflections on the Military Struggle for American Independence*. New York: Oxford University Press, 1976.

Sledge, E. B. *With the Old Breed: At Peleliu and Okinawa*. Novato, CA: Presidio Press, 1981.

Spector, Ronald. *At War, At Sea: Sailors and Naval Warfare in the Twentieth Century*. New York: Viking, 2001.

Spector, Ronald. *Eagle against the Sun: The American War with Japan*. New York: Free Press, 1985.

Symonds, Craig L. *Lincoln and His Admirals: Abraham Lincoln, the U.S. Navy, and the Civil War*. New York: Oxford University Press, 2008.

Taylor, Alan. *American Revolutions: A Continental History, 1750–1804*. New York: W. W. Norton, 2016.

Trask, David F. *The AEF and Coalition Warmaking, 1917–1918*. Lawrence: University Press of Kansas, 1993.

Trask, David F. *The War with Spain in 1898*. New York: Macmillan, 1981.

Trauschweizer, Ingo. *The Cold War U.S. Army: Building Deterrence for Limited War*. Lawrence: University Press of Kansas, 2008.

Watson, Samuel J. *Jackson's Sword: The Army Officer Corps on the Frontier, 1810–1821*. Lawrence: University Press of Kansas, 2012.

Watson, Samuel J. *Peacekeepers and Conquerors: The Army Officer Corps on the Frontier, 1821–1846*. Lawrence: University Press of Kansas, 2013.

Weigley, Russell Frank. *American Way of War: A History of United States Military Strategy and Policy*. New York: Macmillan, 1973.

Weigley, Russell Frank. *History of the United States Army*. Bloomington: Indiana University Press, 1984.

Index

Index

Index